BRITTANY

— *in your pocket* —

MICHELIN

MAIN CONTRIBUTOR: MICHAEL MARRIOTT

PHOTOGRAPH CREDITS
The Travel Library/Stuart Black front cover; back
cover; title page; 5, 7, 9, 11, 13, 14, 15, 17, 19, 20-21,
22, 23, 24, 25, 27(t, b), 28, 29, 30, 33, 34, 36-37, 38,
39, 40, 41, 42, 44, 45, 46, 47, 48, 50, 51, 53, 54-55,
56, 57, 58-59, 61, 62, 65(t), 66, 68, 69(t, b), 70, 70-
71, 72, 72-3, 74-75, 75, 76, 77, 82-83, 87, 88, 89, 90,
91, 92-93, 94, 95, 96-97, 101, 102, 105, 107, 109, 111,
113, 115, 116, 119, 123, 125; The Travel
Library/Stephanie Colasanti 80-81; Bridgeman Art
Library 49; Michael Marriott 64-65, 79.

Front cover: cobbled street in Dinan; back cover: Raz
Point; title page: cat on a windowsill

MANUFACTURE FRANÇAISE DES PNEUMATIQUES MICHELIN

Société en commandite par actions au capital de 2 000 000 000 de francs

Place des Carmes-Déchaux – 63 Clermont-Ferrand (France)

R.C.S. Clermont-Fd 855 200 507

© Michelin et Cie. Propriétaires-Éditeurs 1996

Dépôt légal Mai 97 – ISBN 2-06-630101-9 – ISSN en cours

Printed in Spain 4-97

CONTENTS

Introduction *4*
How to Use this Guide *6*

BACKGROUND
The Five Faces of Brittany
8
Echoes from the Past *12*
The Bretons and the Pardons 20

EXPLORING
BRITTANY
Must See *22*
The Breton Borders *26*
Gazetteer *35*
The Southern Coast *38*
Gazetteer *51*
The Hinterland and the
   Ancient Forest of King
   Arthur *56*
Brittany's Parish Closes 64
Gazetteer *66*
The Channel Coast *68*
Gazetteer *84*
Finistère *86*
Gazetteer *98*

ENJOYING YOUR
VISIT
Weather *100*
Entertainment *100*
Calendar of Events *101*
Food and Drink *103*
Shopping *105*
Sport *106*

A-Z FACTFINDER
The Basics *108*
A-Z Information *110*

Index *127*

INTRODUCTION

Brittany has always been a favourite holiday destination for the French, and it has become increasingly popular among visitors from all over Europe and further afield. The 28 800 sq km (18 000 sq mile) peninsula stands apart from the rest of France. It is a land rich in contrasts and steeped in history and myth, with the Bretons as distinct a people as the land in which they live. The beguiling blend of French and Celtic traditions date back to the 5C.

The most seductive of Brittany's assets is its coastline. Stretching for some 1 200 km (750 miles), it is one of the longest and most varied of any European region. There are beaches glittering with silver sand, necklaces of off-shore islands, half-hidden fishing villages still stubbornly resisting progress, and spectacular rugged cliffs. Inland, Brittany is also a land of contrasts, ranging from the harsh outlines of the dominating granite of the Armorican massif, through heather and gorse-clad windswept moors, to rich meadows and lush fields, dense forests and winding river valleys.

Washed by the waves of the Atlantic and the English Channel on three of its four sides, Brittany is a natural choice for families and outdoor-lovers, and those in search of tranquil scenery dotted with evidence of the past. Few regions in France have more evidence of prehistory, or one swathed in so much legend and folklore. The highlights of the area, such as the curious parish *closes*, the timeless standing stones of Carnac and the mysterious Arthurian forest of Brocéliande, are magical experiences which lure visitors back to Brittany again and again.

There are many pavement cafés where you can sample the Breton specialities.

HOW TO USE THIS GUIDE

A classic Breton plateau de fruits de mer, served up in a Cancale restaurant.

Within a region so rich in contrasts, the whole cannot be absorbed in one trip. It is a land to be explored, savoured and enjoyed at a leisurely pace, perhaps choosing one area, saving the rest for another time.

The guide is divided into four main sections: **Background** sets the scene: Brittany's landscape, its rich history and culture, the legends and heroes.

Exploring Brittany starts with a list of the best 'must see' sights which should be on everyone's holiday checklist. The guide is then divided into five regions: the Breton Borders, The Southern Coast, The Hinterland, The Channel Coast and Finistère. Within each of these regions, we provide a tour of the best and most interesting towns and villages, beaches and landmarks, providing plenty of ideas for excursions and sightseeing. A gazetteer of places not mentioned in detail within the main regions completes each section.

Enjoying Your Visit provides friendly, no-nonsense advice on a some of the day-to-day holiday activities, features that can make the difference between a good holiday or visit and a great one.

A–Z Factfinder is an easy-to-use reference list of practical information on everything from tipping or hiring cars, to using the phone and the currency.

A word of warning: opening hours and telephone numbers change all the time, so it is a good idea to double-check with a local tourist information office when you go there.

THE FIVE FACES OF BRITTANY

Brittany can be broadly divided into Upper Brittany (Haute-Bretagne) and Lower Brittany (Basse-Bretagne). The latter region comprises most of the peninsula and has much stronger Celtic influences.

The landscape is dominated by the rugged coastline, studded with bays and inlets sheltering small fishing ports and sandy bays. Inland, the hills rise to more than 330m (1 000ft) – the highest point is Toussaines Beacon at 384m (1 288ft). These windswept uplands are the much reduced remains of an ancient chain of mountains composed mostly of infertile granites and schists.

Upper Brittany has a gentler landscape, with the great valleys of the Rance in the north and the Loire to the south providing fertile soils for a wide range of crops.

Administratively, Brittany comprises four *départements*: Ille-et-Vilaine, Côtes-d'Armor, Finistère and Morbihan. This guide also includes part of the Loire-Atlantique as far south as Nantes as this has traditionally been part of the region.

For the holiday-maker or visitor, Brittany can most easily be divided into five distinct areas which this guide will follow. The **Breton Borders** is roughly defined as a north-south band along Brittany's inland border embracing the region's capital, Rennes, and sweeping as far south as the Loire valley at Nantes. The region includes several impressive bastions such as Fougères, Vitré and Châteaubriant, and perhaps the

The view from the granite outcrop of Roc Trévezel (384m) is worth the climb.

most spectacular of them all – Mont-St-Michel.

The **southern coast**, with its high sunshine totals, provides a tantalizing hint of the atmosphere of the Riviera, with popular resorts like La Baule in the far south-east. Further west there are splendid beaches along the wild Quiberon Peninsula and at Carnac, also well-known for its enigmatic standing stones.

Then, away from the summer bustle of the beaches and resorts, slumbers the timeless Argoat – inland Brittany. Once densely forested, the present **Hinterland** is mainly pastoral, broken by wide heaths and moorland and criss-crossed by a network of narrow farm lanes. The remote hilltops and wooded valleys combine to create a landscape quite unlike any other to be found in France.

The **Channel Coast** from the Normandy border to Roscoff has a more invigorating climate than the south but is still Brittany's most popular holiday region. Between ports such as St-Malo and Perros-Guirec are rugged headlands composed of the famous rose granite and wide, sandy stretches of beach.

Brittany's far west, known as **Finistère**, still has many miles of untamed and dramatic coastline. The Crozon Peninsula, between Raz Point (Pointe du Raz) and St-Mathieu Point (Pointe de St-Mathieu) is at the heart of this wilder Brittany, where Atlantic breakers crash upon granite after 4 800km (3 000 miles) of uninterrupted progress.

The Quiberon Peninsula lives up to its name – Wild Coast (Côte Sauvage).

ECHOES FROM THE PAST

Early History

When Celtic tribes settled in Brittany in the 5C the strange megaliths, which are still scattered throughout the region, were already ancient. They stand today, imperious of our own age as they were during 400 years of the Roman civilization, during the barbarous Dark Ages which followed, and the long period of the Holy Roman Empire beginning with **Charlemagne**'s conquest of Brittany in 799.

The statue of Bertrand Du Guesclin stands in the Place Du-Guesclin, Dinan.

By this time, the old Celtic name of Armor – Country by the Sea – had been replaced by Bretagne – Little Britain, following mass migration from the British Isles by the persecuted Celts. Early in the 9C, the first of three Breton heroes, **Nominoé**, an ambitious local war-lord, was made Count of Vannes. Within a decade he had united all the old feudal factions into a governable entity. So successful was he, that the boundaries of the subsequent independent duchy remained largely unaltered right up to the French Revolution of 1789. Nominoé is still revered, especially in Dol-de-Bretagne where he eventually had himself crowned king of Brittany, and in Vannes, which he made Brittany's first capital.

During the 10C, the province was brutally impoverished by rampaging Normans, who faced no opposition from the neighbouring kingdom of France, which viewed the duchy indifferently, as a distant satellite with pretentions to be a monarchy in its own right. **Alain Barbe-Torte**, the last crowned head, died in 952, and there followed debilitating feudalism for the next four centuries.

Medieval Brittany

Although not directly involved in the protracted Hundred Years' War between France and England (1337–1453), Brittany produced the second of her great heroes to fight for the French cause, **Bertrand Du Guesclin**. He was such an ugly child that his parents almost disowned him. He grew to become a formidable warrior and a constant

scourge of England's invading armies. Born near Dinan, illiterate and recklessly bold, he was the most honoured of medieval knights. He died in battle in 1380, aged 60 years. His heart rests in St-Sauveur church, Dinan.

The War of Succession was fought in Brittany between the French led by **Charles de Blois** and the English under **Jean de Montfort**. It was finally won by de Montfort at the battle of Auray in 1364, when Du Guesclin was defeated by the English under the formidable **Sir Charles Chandos**.

You can walk or drive round the medieval ramparts of Guérande.

The Ducal Palace of Nantes was extended by the Duchess Anne. Her additions included these tall, ornate Gothic dormer windows.

Duchess Anne

Exhausted by poverty and constant war, for the next century the dukes of Brittany kept a strict and fruitful neutrality. The region prospered markedly as a result, not least as a maritime province. The growing wealth was reflected in grand architecture. France tried several times to annex her nouveau-riche neighbour but was thwarted, by and large, by a third Breton hero – the **Duchess Anne**.

This last ruler of independent Brittany strived persistently to keep her domain for Bretons. She ensured, through the betrothal of her daughter to the future **François I** of France, that the duchy gained fully from the inevitable take-over. This came some 18 years after Anne's death in 1514, at the relatively early age of 37 years. Brittany thus swore allegiance to the French crown, fortuitously, as it happened, since the crowning of François heralded the dawn of that cultural Golden Age, the **Renaissance**. By proclamation, however, the duchy retained its own Breton parliament, army and taxation system.

Brittany as part of France

From that auspicious moment, in 1532, Brittany's fortunes became inextricably entwined with those of France, and Bretons contributed much to the wealth and prestige of the enlarged nation. **Jacques Cartier**, the great navigator, sailed out of St-Malo to discover the St Lawrence seaway into Canada. Meanwhile, periods of peace were enjoyed between those old enemies, France and England, and maritime commerce burgeoned.

Alas, however, this prosperity ended with the **Wars of Religion** between Catholics and Protestants (Huguenots) and in predominantly Catholic Brittany a savage civil war flared up in 1588. Anarchy reigned until a desperately sought peace was secured through the historic **Edict of Nantes**, in 1598. Signed by the King of France, Henri IV, himself a lapsed Protestant, this document commanded freedom for all religious followers.

With **Louis XIV**, the Sun King, upon the throne (1661–1715) France saw a new period of prosperity. National good fortune was reflected in the building of grandiose provincial châteaux and new city centres, and seemingly unending commercial success. Nantes prospered, largely through the slave trade, Brest became the naval power-house of western Europe, while Lorient (L'Orient), was created as the home port of the new French East India Company. St-Malo, in this heady era, was a fortified haven for swashbuckling privateers, granted royal freedom to plunder any foreign ships. Predictably, very little of this new wealth filtered down to the people. On the contrary, swingeing taxes were extorted to refill fast-emptying state coffers and the oppressed Breton peasants revolted.

The ramparts of St-Malo were begun in the 12C, but were added to up to the 18C.

BACKGROUND

French Revolution

In 1675 yet another century and a half of disastrous decline for the province began, insurrections being quelled ruthlessly by royalist forces. The Brittany parliament warred constantly with the central government, while the social and political upheaval which began with the storming of the Paris Bastille in 1789 heralded precious little liberty, fraternity, or equality for the Breton people. Disillusioned by the outcome of the French Revolution, the devout Catholic populace was affronted by the plunder of churches, horrified by the wanton cruelty of the ruling Convention, and reduced to subsistence level by ever more savage taxes. Countless Bretons, with little to lose, reverted to the royalist cause. This army of counter-rebels (Chouans) perished in their thousands in the ensuing uprising, not only in Brittany, but in neighbouring Vendée.

This lovely stained-glass window in the Notre-Dame-du Haut, near Moncontour, is in memory of those who perished in the Great War, 1914-18

Despite smouldering Breton resentment against the Napoleonic regime, the blazing successes of Napoleon could hardly be ignored, with France dominating mainland Europe. Pontivy certainly prospered as the central Brittany headquarters of a vast military project which included the linking of Brest and Nantes by inland canal.

Brittany in Modern Times

Brittany's good fortune was short-lived and, following Napoleon's final defeat, the province became a largely neglected backwater until the **Great War** (1914–18) decimated an already migrating population. More than a quarter of a million Breton soldiers and sailors perished. During the **Second World War** losses were more material, especially around major ports and townships, many of which were devastated.

During the post-war boom that followed, however, Brittany fared well, with rebuilt and massively expanded cities reflecting the new era of industry and affluence, while the hinterland (in part) was rediscovered as a valued source of quarrying and mining wealth. Now, despite the socio-economic uneasiness affecting Europe at the ebb of the 20C, Brittany benefits from an efficient, modern infrastructure.

The Bretons and the Pardons

Still proudly *paysan* at heart, Bretons do not lightly lay aside their age-old culture or traditions, proven by the many religious and folklore festivals so staunchly perpetuated. All across the province, Celtic forefathers are honoured through colourful processions and ceremonies, some dating back to the Druidic period.

Religious celebrations are known as *pardons*, a name deriving from the Catholic Church's tradition of granting indulgences to the penitent on the village or town's saint's day, so that their sins could be pardoned. Nowadays, the religious *pardons* often combine with folk festivals.

There are *pardons* on the grandest of scales in the large towns, but even small villages have more modest, but equally fervent ceremonies. Whichever you choose, you should really try to experience at least one *pardon* during your visit.

After the ceremony in church, a colourful procession follows in the afternoon, often in traditional costume, with singing, banners, flags and candles. The more general festivities then take

Traditional music and costumes feature in Cornouaille Festival.

over, and vary according to the scale of the event.

The Cornouaille Festival is held every July in Quimper when the bards declaim in the timeless *Brezoneg* tongue and the strangely haunting Breton bagpipes skirl. Part-Christian part-pagan, these annual revivals of a long-gone world add a touch of magic which is uniquely Breton. Details are given of some of the main festivals and events on pp.101–103, but you will find local *pardons* all over Brittany.

MUST SEE

Mont-St-Michel★★★

Designated a World Heritage Site, this tiny granite island surmounted by its huge abbey has everything: history, architectural splendour and a magnificent setting.

Carnac★ and the Quiberon Peninsula★

The ancient standing stones at Carnac are one of the world's great man-made mysteries, while the Quiberon Peninsula, with its half-hidden coves, weird rock formations and sandy inlets, is a natural wonder.

Baie des Trépassés (Bay of the Dead), near Raz Point, can be a stormy place in the winter, but during balmy summer weather it shows a quieter side to its nature.

Quimper★★ and Raz Point★★★

The ancient capital of Quimper has a glorious cathedral and medieval streets. At the heart of Breton culture, it is known for its *faïence* (ceramic-ware). West lies Raz Point, the most awesome spot in Brittany.

The Hinterland Heart

Josselin, with its Renaissance-style **castle★★**, **Guerlédan Lake★★** with its walks and watersports, and **Paimpont Forest★** with its echoes of King Arthur give a taste of the Argoat's varied attractions.

La Baule★★★ and Brière Regional Nature Park★★★

A huge sandy beach, plush hotels, pine-shaded villas and a great promenade for people-watching make La Baule one of the most fashionable of Brittany's resorts, while in contrast, Brière, just inland, is one of France's biggest wildlife reserves.

Josselin Castle stands majestic on the banks of the river Oust.

Morlaix★
Pleasure craft now bob on their moorings at the centre of this old-time commercial port, set dramatically beneath its huge 19C viaduct, and the steeply terraced streets are redolent of the town's swashbuckling past.

Perros-Guirec★★
A family resort *par excellence*, with amenities for all tastes, Perros-Guirec is the ideal base for exploring the Pink Granite Coast.

The Parish Closes★★
Concentrated in western Finistère, these old churchyards with their elaborate triumphal arches, ossuaries and calvaries are a unique feature of Brittany.

The colourful Festival of Cornouaille, in Quimper, is typical of festivals held throughout Brittany.

Vannes★★ and the Morbihan Gulf★★

Ramparts, fortress towers and medieval wash-houses are features of this ancient city tumbling down to its river port. The island-studded Morbihan Gulf, of which Vannes is the acknowledged capital, provides endless outdoor activities.

St-Malo★★★

Guardian of the head of the Rance estuary for centuries, St-Malo is a treasure-trove of maritime history with its great citadel and yacht basins. Its fortified heart, seemingly untouched by time, was perfectly restored after war damage in 1944.

The narrow streets of the Old Town in Vannes are crammed with interesting shops and stalls.

EXPLORING BRITTANY

THE BRETON BORDERS

Largely consisting of the Ille-et-Vilaine
département, stretching from the Gulf of St-
Malo southwards to the Loire river, this
former frontier country between eastern
Brittany and the rest of France is studded
with medieval fortresses that testify to its
turbulent past. Pastoral and peaceful today,
the gentle landscape is criss-crossed with tiny
lanes linking farms and hamlets, but by
contrast it encompasses the conurbations of
Rennes, regional capital of Brittany today,
and Nantes, the province's former capital.

Mont-St-Michel★★★
Mont-St-Michel lies within Normandy, just,
but no visitor to Brittany should miss this
granite island rising out of the wide shifting
sands of St-Michel's Bay. It is reached by a
2km (1 mile) causeway.

The mount's great glory is its **abbey**, first
established as a monastic site in the 8C when
the Archangel Michael came to Aubert,
Bishop of Avranches, in a vision and told
him to build a sanctuary here. The island
soon became a place of pilgrimage and new
buildings were erected over the centuries,
creating the Romanesque and Gothic
architectural masterpiece seen today.

From the 13C the island was fortified; a
walk along the ramparts gives good views of
the bay. Grande-Rue, lined with 15–16C
houses, shops and restaurants, winds
through the town that grew up at the base of
the rock. Additional attractions are the
Archéoscope (a special-effects tour of the
island's history), **St Peter's Parish Church**
(Église paroissiale St-Pierre) and the house
(1365) of Breton war-lord Bertrand Du

*Mont-St-Michel is a
magical sight in the
quiet of dusk.*

The steep and narrow Grand-Rue of Mont-St-Michel is a lively and busy thoroughfare lined with souvenir shops.

Guesclin (*see* p.13), **Logis Tiphaine,** named after his wife Tiphaine.

Fougères★★ to Nantes★★★

To the south of Mont-St-Michel, extending to the Loire river, is the string of castles built in the Middle Ages to reinforce the natural barrier of wild marshland and guard the province from invasion from France. Of these castles, **Fougères★★** is the most formidable and one of the largest in western Europe. Rising from its granite knoll, the fortress, constructed on the site of an earlier stronghold built by the Breton Duke Raoul II in the 12C, guarded the only all-weather pilgrim route from Chartres. Seldom were castles of the Middle Ages conceived on such a scale and though now largely a ruin, 13 of the massive towers – the most imposing

Although the keep of Fougères Castle was razed in 1166 by King Henry II of England, the walls and 13 of its towers have remained intact.

s you walk along
he rampart, or
vander around
nside the castle at
'itré, you can
magine some of the
attles that were
ought here over the
enturies.

of which is the **Tour Mélusine** – still rise
above the moat waters. There is access to an
interesting rampart walk, while parking
space can usually be found in Place Raoul II.

Across the river, on higher ground, is the
medieval town, with its handsome half-
timbered houses centred around the ancient
cattle market and attractive **public gardens**.
Colourful café life can be found in and
around Place Aristide-Briand, and Place du
Théâtre. Impressionist painter Emmanuel
de la Villéon was born in the town, and the
museum (**Musée de la Villéon**) is devoted to
his work. Formerly the shoe-making capital
of France, Fougères is now a thriving centre
for high-tech industry.

Some 30km (19 miles) south of Fougères
is an equally stunning castle at **Vitré★★**,
consisting of a cluster of 13C towers with
pepper-pot roofs above blue-schist stone
ramparts. In the **Argenterie Tower** the
region's natural history is displayed, and in

the **St Lawrence Tower** (Tour St-Laurent) is a museum of 15C and 16C sculpture.

Surrounding the castle is one of Brittany's best-preserved old towns. Park on the spacious castle apron by the tourist office and stroll along Rue de la Baudrairie and Rue Poterie to enjoy the striking, individually-styled town houses built by merchants made rich from sailcloth produced from local hemp from the 15C to 17C. Today, atmospheric cafés and restaurants add a lively touch to this picture-postcard town, making it a favoured base in eastern Ille-et-Vilaine, not least since Rennes (*see* p.37) is only 35km (22 miles) west.

Just 7km (4½ miles) south of Vitré is the **Rochers-Sévigné Château**. This was the home of the Marquise de Sévigné in the 17C, whose witty letters to her daughter were later published. They provide an entertaining insight into French provincial life at that time. The garden was designed by Le Nôtre and there is parkland beyond.

La Roche-aux-Fées, consisting of 42 purple schist stones, is one of the most important megalithic sites in Brittany.

After Vitré, Brittany's largest megalithic monument awaits the southbound traveller. **La Roche-aux-Fées★**, meaning Fairies' Rock, lies west of La Guerche surrounded by trees. This curious pile of enormous boulders – possibly a 4 000-year-old neolithic tomb – is cloaked in Breton legend, which the locals of nearby **Guerche-de-Bretagne**, a market town and *Station Verte*, are happy to recount. Rambling and angling are popular in this pastoral area, where the pace of life is slow.

Continuing south, sleepy, half-timbered villages and towns welcome visitors and dispense *cidre artisanal*, goats' cheese and traditional cuisine. **Châteaubriant**, the only large town between Rennes and Nantes, boasts fortress defences that ensured independence until 1532. The original part of the **castle**, built in the 11C on the banks of the Chère, is a gaunt, broken-toothed ruin now; the Renaissance buildings designed by Jean de Laval, a Governor of Brittany in the 16C, are considerably better preserved, though less evocative.

The sprawl of modern Châteaubriant is not so impressive, but the **Carrière des Fusillés**, 2km (1 mile) away, is a sombre memorial to victims of the Second World War. The base is built with earth taken from execution grounds.

South-east of Châteaubriant, in the wide valley of the Loire at a strategic Roman ford, is **Ancenis**. Here, crouched below vineyard slopes (France's most northerly), is yet another castle. An important link in the frontier chain, Anciens was persistently assaulted in the Middle Ages because of its location; it has been well restored.

South of Nantes, you enter Muscadet country, where there is much to attract the active explorer. Nearby **Vallet** is the heart of local wine-making (vineyard tours arranged), while **Le Pallet** was the birthplace of Pierre Abélard in 1079, to whom there is a small museum. Abélard, a gifted philosopher, was brutally castrated for secretly marrying the much younger Héloïse who was of noble birth and had conceived a son before their marriage. After this tragic event, they both took holy orders. The letters they exchanged record one of the world's great love stories.

The final link in the defence chain along the Breton borders is **Clisson**. Here the powerful 13C **castle** stands as another romantic ruin, while the town itself – razed by Chouan rebels during The Terror – was rebuilt by a devout admirer of Italian Renaissance style, with Italianate terraces blending oddly but somehow successfully with Breton solidity. The 15C timber-covered market is, however, decidedly French.

Built near the Sèvre river, the semi-rural market town possesses a magnificent Romanesque churches, a fine Gothic bridge and wooded château grounds. It is a good base from which to explore Brittany's one real metropolis and former capital, Nantes.

Nantes★★★

Much of the city of **Nantes**, one of the greatest industrial and commercial river port conurbations in western France, is not really tourist terrain, but happily the jewels of the past are confined to a compact square kilometre on the north bank of the Loire. The centre is best seen on foot or from public transport (early-birds might find car parking spaces in Place Maréchal-Foch, among the 18C merchant mansions) and options include mini-coach, tramway and tourist-train sightseeing trips from the tourist office.

It was the Romans under Caesar who first developed the crude Celtic settlement into a huge fortified harbour and through succeeding centuries whalers, slavers and tall ships of the sugar-cane trade set sail on countless quests for wealth, with Nantes reaching the zenith of its prosperity in the early 18C.

Dominating the old quarter is the

The imposing façade of St Peter's and St Paul's Cathedral, Nantes, showing the splendid Flamboyant window.

towering 15C **St Peter's and St Paul's Cathedral** (Cathédrale St-Pierre et St-Paul), the soaring Flamboyant masterpiece containing the tomb of François II, father of Duchess Anne (*see* p.15). The old town hub, around **Place du Bouffay** (the city's oldest square), is deservedly popular. Don't miss the **Maison des Palefrois** (ancient stables), and the **Maison des Apothicaires**, in the 15C Place du Change.

The 15C **Ducal Castle** (Château des Ducs de Bretagne), home of Duchesse Anne, epitomizes the glory of Breton history, and i

The main building inside the Ducal Castle, Nantes.

was here that the enlightened Edict of
Nantes was signed in 1598 (*see* p.16). Today,
the castle is a quiet oasis of ramparted lawns,
formal gardens and gentle moat waters. The
palace houses the **Museum of Local Folk Art**
(Musée d'Art populaire régional) with
Breton costumes, models and furniture.

Beyond the ancient seat of Brittany's
dukes, the **Museum of Fine Arts** (Musée des
Beaux-Arts) displays masterpieces by
Tintoretto and Courbet, while in the Rue de
l'Hermitage is the **Jules Verne Museum**
(Musée Jules-Verne). Verne (renowned for
his science fiction novels) was born here in
1828. Nantes' **Botanical Gardens** (Jardin des
Plantes) are also celebrated and popular
with lunchtime picnickers in summer.

GAZETTEER

Antrain – 20km (13 miles) south of Mont-St-Michel

This little hill town, its steep streets lined
with 16C and 17C houses, looks down on the
Couesnon river. Just to the south (2km/
1 mile) is **Bonne-Fontaine Castle** (Château
de Bonne-Fontaine), a restored manor
house with splendid parkland.

Bais – 15km (9 miles) south of Vitré

This interesting hilltop market town has a
16C Gothic church with a porch with three
pediments – known as the 'Lepers' Porch' –
over a Renaissance doorway with twin doors.
About 5km (3 miles) south is **Lake Carcraon**
(Étang Carcraon), popular with anglers.

Château de la Motte-Glain – 17km (11 miles) north-east of La Meilleraye

This imposing Renaissance manor house was

modernized from a 15C stronghold. It is surrounded by woodland and stands by a lake.

Combourg★ – 40km (25 miles) south-west of Mont-St-Michel

This pretty town is famous for its associations with François-René de Chateaubriand (1768–1848), the famous French writer and statesman. For two years he lived in the gloomy medieval **castle** which stands by an ornamental lake at the edge of the town. The haunted **Cat Tower** (Tour du Chat), which housed Chateaubriand's bedroom, is now a museum of his life and work. Also of interest in the town is the 16C **Lantern House** (Maison de la Lanterne), built to illuminate the street.

Dol-de-Bretagne★ – 25km (16 miles) south-west of Mont-St-Michel

Formerly a bishopric and one of several starting points for the traditional pilgrimage of Brittany's cathedrals made by Bretons in the Middle Ages, Dol stands on the edge of an inland 'cliff'. Old timbered houses can be seen near the impressive **cathedral**, and the **museum** (musée) of the town is housed in the treasury.

    Mont-Dol, 2km (1 mile) north of Dol, is a granite hill

offering sweeping views of St-Michel Bay.

Rennes **

Brittany's regional capital, Rennes is a modern commercial agglomeration with limited tourist appeal and only a fraction of the historic wealth of Nantes, the original Breton capital (*see* p.32). A catastrophic fire in 1720 wiped out the best of the Celtic city and, even when rebuilt, Flaubert described Rennes in 1846 as, 'a place of no interest'. The Second World War led to further, massive damage.

Having said this, part of the **old town** (Vieux Rennes) did survive and this includes the 15C **Church of St-Germain**, odd rampart fragments and some half-timbered 16C houses in Rue St-Georges and Rue de la Psalette. There are, too, the 15C main city gates, the **Mordelaises Gates** (Portes Mordelaises), and **Tour Duchesne** in Rue Nantaise.

When the sun shines, the **Thabor Gardens** (Jardin du Thabor) are ideal for a picnic lunch. In not so clement weather try the **Museum of Brittany** (Musée de Bretagne) and **Museum of Fine Arts** (Musée des Beaux-Arts), both housed in the former university on Quai Emile-Zola.

Half-timbered buildings in Rennes.

THE SOUTHERN COAST

The Atlantic coastline of Brittany, from St-Nazaire to Concarneau, may not be as rugged and wild as the north coast, but its sunny climate, sandy beaches – fashionable and otherwise – estuaries and inlets have a charm of their own. Handsome old towns, prehistoric remains and the island-studded Morbihan Gulf, where there are boat trips galore, all add to the appeal.

One of the most impressive ways to approach the south coast is from St-Brevin, via the St-Nazaire toll bridge, an awesome structure 2.5km (1½ mile) long, spanning the Loire estuary. Totally rebuilt after the

La Baule lives up to its reputation as one of the most popular resorts in Brittany.

Second World War, visitors should proceed straight to La Baule which lies just 16km (10 miles) away.

Known as the Nice of the North, **La Baule★★★** really does justify its tag: it is at once brash yet exclusive, seasonally crowded, expensive and quite irresistible. There are still traces of *belle époque* buildings among the pines and manicured gardens, but the town is dominated by dazzling, modern hotels, apartments and classy shopping arcades. The harbour is crammed with luxury yachts and the promenade lines a magnificent 9km (5½ mile) golden beach. La Baule has excellent facilities for family holidays, as well as being one of Brittany's most exclusive resorts.

There is always something interesting to watch at the bustling harbour of Le Croisic.

There are countless restaurants and café-bars in La Baule, from the grandest gourmet establishments to fast-food *crêperies*, through every kind of ethnic speciality eating house. For those with money to burn, there is a grand casino and a race course at **Pornichet★**.

Natural attractions on the **Guérande Peninsula★** just to the west include the woodland paths above **Le Pouliguen★** – a former fishing village, the historic salt marshes and coastal walks. The bustling fishing harbour at **Le Croisic★** is backed by 17C houses and the **Océarium** (marine information centre) is fascinating. Here, fish can be seen from a huge transparent tunnel which runs through the seawater pool. A scenic coastal corniche road runs to Le Croisic Point.

To the north of La Baule, the **Grande Brière★**, also known as the Grande Brière Mottière, belongs to the Brière Regional Nature Park. This vast tract of preserved marsh (*marais*) may be explored by traditional boat (*chalan*), by bicycle, on foot via the GR3 long-distance trail, or even partially by car. The 15C walled town of **Guérande★** is a suitable base on the western perimeter of the park.

A windmill in the Brière Regional Nature Park.

Vannes★★

Westwards along the coast is **Vannes**. This is the acknowledged centre for the Morbihan Gulf region and is well geared to tourism, with a leisure zone, **Parc du Golfe**, on the town outskirts. Here there are two museums, one devoted to automated characters, the

Automata Centre (Palais des Automates), and the other to butterflies, the **Live Butterfly Centre** (La Papillonneraie), plus a huge aquarium, **Oceanographic and Tropical Aquarium** (Aquarium océanographique et tropical), which is popular on rainy days.

The ancient capital of Brittany offers culture, the gastronomic pleasures typical of all Breton towns, plus the scenic stimulation of the gulf itself. Vannes is a compact,

The Château de l'Hermine, Vannes, with its colourful gardens, is built into the ramparts.

medieval cobweb of narrow streets filled
with the riches of the past. It is dominated by
the **ramparts** (remparts) and castle
remnants around the principal **Constable
Tower** (Tour du Connétable). The constable
in question was Oliver de Clisson, briefly
incarcerated here in the 14C. **St Peter's
Cathedral** (Cathédrale St-Pierre), dating
from the 13C, is somewhat severe Gothic,
but there is a striking rotunda chapel. Close
by are some of the most picturesque legacies

of Morbihan's capital: Place Henri-IV; Rue St-Salomon; and Rue des Halles, where **La Cohue**, an ancient covered market, has been converted to house the town's museums.

In Rue St-Guenhaël, a 14C dwelling has survived, and in Rue Noë the **House of Vannes** sports gargoyles of a jolly peasant couple, 'Vannes and his Wife'. The **Morbihan Archaeological Museum** (Musée archéologique du Morbihan), in the old Parliament building, has a splendid collection of local prehistoric artefacts; there is also a Breton art museum. Two of the town's most famous landmarks are the medieval **wash-houses** (Vieux Lavoirs), and the **Prison Gate**, with machiolations for dropping unpleasant things on invaders.

The waters of the **Morbihan Gulf★★** are a magnet to walkers and cyclists who enjoy circumnavigating the natural harbour, or those who simply love watersports. Fleets of fast ferries ply between all the major islands – havens of tranquillity with their sandy beaches, woods and those haunting landmarks, the megaliths. **Ile d'Arz**, for example, is studded with standing stones, while the minuscule isle of **Gavrinis** boasts an enormous and mysterious cairn complex, the **Gavrinis Tumulus★★** (Cairn de Gavrinis).

Larmor-Baden is the ferry point for Gavrinis, while Ile d'Arz and Ile-aux-Moines, much appreciated by small-boat sailors and wind-surfers, are served by launches from Quai de la Rabine, not far from Vannes.

Falguérec-en-Séné Nature Reserve, 10km (6 miles) south of Vannes, has been established as a haven for wildfowl on the old salt marshes.

On the seaward side of the gulf, on the Rhuys Peninsula (Presqu'île de Rhuys), is

The famous wash-houses at Vannes have most unusual roofing.

13C **Suscinio Castle**★ (Château de Suscinio).
The Duc de Richemont, victor in the final
battle of the Hundred Years' War, was born
here; his statue stands in Place Maurice-
Marchais in Vannes. This enduring fortress
was breached by Bertrand Du Guesclin (*see*
p.13) in 1373 and the English garrison was
massacred. At the end of the peninsula is
Caesar's Mound, supposed vantage point of
the emperor when the Celtic *Veneti* fleet was
destroyed by Roman war galleys; it is still a
good viewpoint.

*The moated
entrance to Suscinio
Castle, where the
Duc de Richmont
was born.*

Auray to Concarneau

Just west of Vannes is **Auray★**, but despite its historic past (the battle fought here in 1364 ended the War of Succession) and the picturesque quayside of St-Goustan where Benjamin Franklin strode in 1776, it is **Ste-Anne-d'Auray★**, some 6km (4 miles) north, which attracts the crowds. Tens of thousands

The Basilica of Ste-Anne d'Auray was built in the Renaissance style in the 19C.

of pilgrims converge here each July on the *Grand Pardon*, dedicated to Saint Anne, mother of Mary and the patron saint of Brittany (*see* p.103).

A massive 19C basilica and convent stands here, beside what is arguably the most imposing **Great War Memorial** (Monument aux morts) in western France, and where, it is said, Saint Anne appeared in a peasant's vision in 1623.

Carnac★, south of Auray, is famous for its huge megaliths that remain as much a mystery as England's Stonehenge. North of the village, over 1 000 standing stones make up the **Ménec Alignments** (Alignements du Ménec) which are over 1km (½ mile) long. **St-Michel Tumulus**, nearer the village, is a mound of stones and earth covering burial

The megaliths at Carnac are a popular tourist attraction, but they have a strange and haunting beauty if visited at a quieter time.

The beach at Port-Louis has clean, fine sand and inviting waters.

chambers and chests, and the **Museum of Prehistory** (Musée de Préhistoire) contains many of the finds from this site.

Today, Carnac is also a top-class seaside resort these days, and **Carnac-Plage★** boasts all the holiday amenities, along with a sea-bathing centre and a wide choice of caravan and chalet accommodation. (*See* p.51 and p.54 for Quiberon and Belle-Île.)

West of Carnac lies **Lorient**, France's second largest fishing port after Boulogne. Architecturally bland – a legacy of total post-war rebuilding – it was originally created as the home port of the East India Company. The fishing harbour at Kéroman is full of interest, but the nearby submarine base is out of bounds. Across the Blavet river is **Port-Louis★**, with its stark citadel built by Vauban. At one time used as a prison, it now houses several museums. Ferries cross regularly between Lorient and Port-Louis and to offshore **Groix Island★** (Ile de Groix), 45 minutes away, a favourite haunt of skin-divers. The **Groix Island Museum** (Écomusée de L'Ile de Groix) explains the island's history and geography.

Next is **Quimperlé★**, a charming old town situated where the rivers Ellé and Isole meet to form the waters of the Laïta. Split into two parts, Higher and Lower, the town has two medieval churches: 13C and 15C **Notre-**

The Devil's Rocks (Rochers du Diable), on the river Ellé, are a short drive from Quimperlé.

Gauguin's The Vision after the Sermon, *1888, shows Breton women in traditional costume.*

Dame-de-l'Assomption, also known as St-Michel, and 12C **Ste-Croix**, once used by Crusaders. Rue Dom-Morice and Rue Brémond-d'Ars have interesting 15C dwellings. The **Archers' House** (Maison des Archers), in the former, reconstructs the life of the archers who once lived there, and includes a local museum.

A pretty, minor road runs south from Quimperlé through Carnoët Forest to **Le Pouldu** on the coast. For a while Paul Gauguin lived here with his friends in an inn, **Maison Marie Henri**, which they decorated. The interior has been reconstructed in a house nearby, which can be visited.

However, it is to the west, at the old river port of **Pont-Aven★**, that Gauguin and his disciples (later known as the Pont-Aven School) most frequently gathered. Art galleries proliferate here and way-marked walks link the locations of famous paintings. The **museum** houses a collection by the Pont-Aven School, temporary exhibits and a history of the town. Despite the crowds in

summer, Pont-Aven has retained an intimate, 19C ambience; old-fashioned Bélon oysters, cider and *crêpes* are served in the many cafés and restaurants. There are also some very pleasant circular walks in the neighbourhood, and cycle hire is readily available.

Neighbouring **Concarneau**★★ rivals Lorient as a commercial fishing port, but it is a world away visually. Vauban strengthened the **Walled Town** (Ville Close), a fortified island linked to the mainland by two small bridges, for Louis XIV. The parapet walk is a must, as is the **Fishing Museum** (Musée de la Pêche), if only for the original sardine tins on show. The famous early-morning **fish**

The charming harbour at Pont-Aven, once a busy port, is now mainly used by pleasure boats.

There are views of the inner harbour and fishing fleet from the ramparts at Concarneau.

auction (*la criée*) is often pure theatre, enhancing the atmosphere of this colourful old harbour.

The historic gems of Concarneau are complemented by an excellent and safe beach, **Plage des Sables Blancs**, 1km (½ mile) away. This whole great bay, between Concarneau and **Bénodet★★**, an estuary resort, is now holiday Brittany with a vengeance, though happily not at the expense of the natural coastal beauty.

GAZETTEER

Belle-Île★★ – south of the Quiberon Peninsula
This is Brittany's largest offshore island, measuring 17km (11 miles) in length. Its main town, **Le Palais**, is where visitors from Quiberon (*see* p.54) disembark. Here the **Vauban Citadel** (Citadelle Vauban), reached by a mobile footbridge over the lock, houses an historical museum.

The island was once the domain of the wily Fouquet, finance minister of Louis XIV. It was later favoured by actress Sarah Bernhardt and painter Claude Monet.

Inland is largely a bare plateau, but green valleys cut down to the coast and the **Port-Coton Needles** (Aiguilles de Port-Coton) – jagged rocks on the southern shore – are spectacular, as are the **Pointe des Poulains** and the **Grotte de l'Apothicairerie** (though the latter is now closed to the public as the caves are unsafe).

Fouesnant – 15km (9 miles) south-east of Quimper

Cherry and apple orchards surround the town of Fouesnant in this exceptionally fertile area south of Quimper, where potent Breton cider is made.

Just to the south of Fouesnant is the tiny port of **Beg-Meil★**, at the mouth of the Baie de la Forêt, surrounded by sand dunes, pines and pathways. A seasonal ferry operates from here across the bay to Concarneau (*see* p.50) and south to the Iles de Glénan.

Hennebont – 10km (6 miles) north-east of Lorient

Once fortified, this old river port at the head of the Blavet estuary still boasts 13C ramparts which take 1½ hours to walk around. A multi-arched bridge spans the river and a 16C Gothic church towers over the wide expanse of Place Maréchal-Foch. Millions of sardine tins were once made in Hennebont, but new technology has now superseded steel forging.

Hennebont is the horse-breeding capital of Morbihan and its stud farm (*haras national*) can be visited.

tower and fortified walls still remain standing at Largoët Castle, along with an impressive 14C keep.

Elven Towers★ – 14km (9 miles) north-east of Vannes

Also known as **Largoët Castle** (Forteresse de Largoët), this glorious feudal remnant was once the domain of Duchess Anne's tutor. It was razed by Charles VIII of France in the 15C. The parkland is the setting for *son-et-lumière* shows in summer, when the past is magically evoked.

Pornic★ – 25km (16 miles) south of St-Nazaire

A slightly old-fashioned air pervades this small-boat haven and deep-water harbour backed by farmland between the Vendée boundary and the Loire estuary. The gaunt remains of a 13C and 14C castle at nearby **Machecoul** form a sinister landmark. It was once owned by Gilles de Rais (1404–1440), a companion of Joan of Arc and the original 'Bluebeard', who was eventually hanged in Nantes for hideous crimes.

Quiberon★ – Quiberon Peninsula

The peninsula juts out to the south of Carnac. Popular because of its proximity to the Côte Sauvage on the western side of the peninsula, and its sandy beach, the resort of Quiberon is also a busy fishing port and hydrotherapy centre. Ferries operate from Port Maria to Belle-Île (*see* p.51).

La Roche-Bernard – 27km (17 miles) northeast of La Baule

Situated on the northern edge of the Brière Regional Nature Park, this promontory town commands the heights above the wide Vilaine river. It was a Protestant enclave in the Middle Ages and has endured a long and violent history. The first triple-deck warship was built here in the 17C in what was one of the busiest wooden-shipyards in France. There is still a colourful quayside, while part of **Chapelle Notre-Dame** survives from the 11C. Beside the suspension bridge (1960) and a more modern bridge built in the 1990s, a section of the 19C version, dynamited by the Germans in 1944, remains. The town is now a pleasure-boat centre offering excellent watersports and visitor facilities.

There are some popular beaches on the Quiberon Peninsula.

THE HINTERLAND

The interior of Brittany, known as the Argoat (land of woods), is less well known and less crowded than the coastal regions. Paimpont Forest, the ancient Brocéliande Forest of King Arthur and his knights, which once stretched between Rennes and Huelgoat, is a place of myths so powerful that they are held to be nearer truth than legend by Bretons. At the heart of the hinterland, around Pontivy, there is tangible Napoleonic history amid a world of quiet waterways and lakes. Further west, Armorique is a region of ancient wooded ravines and moorland heights.

Paimpont to Guerlédan Lake

A settlement since the 7C, **Paimpont** is a forest village, distinguished by a huge 17C abbey overlooking a tranquil lake. Two long-distance trails converge here, along with shorter local walks. Of the original Brocéliande Forest, only some 43 sq km (27 sq miles) of the **forest of Paimpont★** survive, but it is a place of mystery, long sacred to the

Detail of King Arthur at the famous Round Table, from a window in the church at Tréhorenteuc.

Celts, with many unexpected treasures.

One of these is the **Barenton Fountain** (Fontaine de Barenton), near the hamlet of Folle-Pensée. It was said that whenever water fell on to the nearby rock, **Merlin's Step** (Perron de Merlin), wild storms followed. Close to **Tréhorenteuc** village is the eerie **Valley of No Return** (Val sans Retour), accessible to walkers only. This secret dale is where Morgana the witch lured her ex-lovers – including Merlin (Arthur's sorceror) – to an eternal prison. In the local church are images of the Holy Grail and the Court of Arthur at the fabled Round Table.

North of Paimpont, the **Château de Comper** is claimed to be the birthplace of the enchantress Viviane, the beautiful Lady

The 14C Château de Trécesson, near Paimpont, is surrounded by a moat.

of the Lake who raised Lancelot, Knight of
the Round Table. The château is now an
Arthurian museum.

From Paimpont, a popular tour takes in
Josselin, Malestroit and Rochefort-en-Terre.
Josselin★★ has a fairytale Renaissance castle
which rises above the river Oust. Its elegant
tower cappings and delicate dormer
windows cannot disguise the stern medieval
ramparts below the battlements first razed in

the 12C. This castle has a bloody history; not least its connection with the Battle of the Thirty, fought in 1351 during the War of Succession, when a group of 30 knights slaughtered each other in personal combat. An obelisk marks the spot nearby.

Seat of the powerful Rohan family to this day, the interior of the château is equally interesting for its furniture and paintings and a collection of historic dolls (**Musée des Poupées**) displayed in the castle stables. Visitors should devote a full day to Josselin and the old town. Look out for the Gothic church of **Our Lady of the Brambles** (Basilique Notre-Dame-du-Roncier).

Malestroit, which also lies on the Oust river and the Nantes–Brest canal, is one of the most attractive market towns in Morbihan. There are many 16C and 17C houses to delight and surprise here, as well as cobbled streets and carved façades.

At **St-Marcel**, 3km (2 miles) west, amid what was remote Lanvaux terrain during the Second World War, the Maquis guerillas had a secret stronghold. Today, the forested enclosure is an open-air re-creation of occupied Brittany and includes the **Museum of Breton Resistance** (Musée de la Résistance Bretonne). There is an adventure playground and picnic area nearby.

Across the moorland of Lanvaux ridge – which extends east to west for nearly 40km (25 miles) – is **Rochefort-en-Terre★**. Here, along a ravine bluff on the historic Route des Ducs heritage trail, the ruins of a 14C **castle** tower over a cluster of lovingly restored 17C dwellings, as photogenic as it is welcoming to hikers traversing the GR38 moorland trail.

About 3km (2 miles) east of Rochefort, at

Cruising along the Nantes–Brest canal a relaxed and leisurely way to take in the sights.

Malansac, is the **Prehistoric Park** (Parc de Préhistoire). Here, fascinating tableaux depict life as it was for ancient Bretons some 4 000 years ago. Reconstructions include hunting scenes of long-extinct species, and the method by which the region's mighty standing stones may have been transported.

To the north of the Lanvaux ridge is **Pontivy**, a small town with two contrasting faces: the medieval area with timbered houses below the 15C **castle** ramparts, and the grid-pattern town with its barracks and grand public buildings created by Napoleon in 1805. He chose to make Pontivy the military centre of Brittany (it was known then as Napoléonville) since it lay mid-way between the ports of Brest and Nantes after they were linked by canalizing the Blavet river. Pontivy has all the amenities of a major market town and is a good touring base for the area.

Further north along the course of the Blavet river is **Guerlédan Lake★★** (Lac de Guerlédan). Brittany's largest lake (15km/9 miles long), it was created by damming the Blavet in the 1920s, but looks completely natural. Boating and watersports facilities are available.

West of the lake, a stretch of the Nantes–Brest canal towpath invites some gentle cycling, while cliff-like granite outcrops covered with mixed woodland add variety to the GR 37 hiking trail and local waymarked footpaths. One of these routes leads to a glorious 12C Cistercian abbey ruin (**Abbaye de Bon-Repos**) at the western end of the lake. The nearby **Bon-Repos Lock** (Écluse de Bon-Repos), by an old pack-horse bridge, is another interesting feature.

There are ample car park and picnic areas

This pavement café in Pontivy is a riot of colour, adorned with flowers.

all around the lake and a comprehensive sport and leisure complex close to **Mur-de-Bretagne,** at the eastern end. Just to the north of the town, in woodland, is the 17C **Ste-Suzanne Chapel**, a favourite subject of the landscape painter Corot (1796–1875) long before the lake existed.

South of Guerlédan Lake is **Quénécan Forest** (Forêt de Quénécan), some 2 500ha (6 175 acres) where wild boar and deer roam. The forest consists of pine and heathland with swathes of beech and spruce around Lake Fourneau (Étang du Fourneau). The hamlet of **Les Forges des Salles** was the site of an iron and steel industry in the 18C and 19C.

Carhaix-Plouguer to the Armorique Regional Nature Park

Between this appealing region of woods, water and plentiful holiday amenities, and the Armorique Regional Nature Park to the west, there is an empty wilderness that has remained unchanged for centuries: this includes the lonely heath south of Carhaix-Plouguer and the **Roc de Toulaëron**, at 326m (1 045ft) the high point of the **Noires Mountains★★** (Les Montagnes Noires) and a good viewpoint.

Carhaix-Plouguer is a pleasant market town, medieval in part but also proud of its Roman legacy, the once-mighty Pont Gaulois aqueduct. The well-preserved 15C **House of the Seneschal** (Maison du Sénéchal) in Rue Brizeux is well worth visiting, and its conversion from provincial governor's residence to tourism office has been sympathetically achieved. Watered by the Aulne river and canalized in part, this is good cycling country with a choice of colour-coded circuit routes.

Cycling, particularly mountain biking, is also popular around **Huelgoat★★**, a resort which attracts walkers and backpackers. Once a silver mining town, it sits amid forested hills and spectacular ravine water courses. Excellent leisure amenities make this a good base from which to enjoy excursions into the surrounding countryside.

Walkers can discover fascinating beauty spots such as **Artu's Camp** (Camp d'Artus), thought to be Roman until it was proven Celtic by Sir Mortimer Wheeler, the English archaeologist (1890–1976). There is also the **Logan Stone** (Roche Tremblante), a 100 000kg monster which can be rocked easily by hand, and other natural wonders such as the **Devil's Grotto** (Grotte du Diable), **Mill Rocks** (Chaos du Moulin) and the **Amphitheatre** (Théâtre de Verdure).

Some of the most celebrated of Brittany's parish closes (*see* p.64) are located in and around the eastern part of the **Armorique Regional Nature Park**, such as Pleyben and St-Thégonnec. Almost equidistant from these two closes is one of Brittany's most remote, **Commana**. Beside the 16C hill-village church there is a particularly fine example of religious sculpture amid pastoral surroundings.

Commana is quite near an even older hallowed place, the granite landmark of **Roc Trévezel**, some 384m (1 260ft) above sea level, reached by a pilgrim path. Sweeping panoramas over a timeless Brittany hinterland are the walker's reward for a steep climb.

The Boars' Pool (Mare aux Sangliers) in the Huelgoat forest gets its name from the huge boulders which resemble boars' heads in shape.

Brittany's Parish Closes

A visit to Brittany is not complete without at least one visit to a parish close, a group of religious monuments centred around the church and cemetery. Often, villages competed with each other, trying to out-do their neighbours, resulting in many splendid structures in rela-

tively small towns and villages.

All parish closes have the same basic elements, though designs vary. The entrance to the cemetery often takes the form of a **triumphal arch**, symbolizing immortality for the Just. The **ossuary** or **charnel house** is built to house the bones of those exhumed to

make room for new graves when the churchyard became full. The **calvary** is a monument, sometimes quite simple, but often elaborately carved, showing scenes of the Passion and Crucifixion. These were once used as a teaching aid by the priest, who would preach next to the calvary, using the sculptures to illustrate his teachings.

Three of the most celebrated of Brittany's parish closes are located in and around the eastern part of the Armorique Regional Nature Park. The small market town of **Pleyben★★** has one of the oldest and most complex; the calvary depicts not only the Last Supper but the ceremonial washing of the disciples' feet. The tree-shaded ossuary is mid-16C. There is wonderfully detailed sculpture, too, at the most celebrated Breton close, **St-Thégonnec★★**, on the northern park boundary. This splendid trio of calvary, ossuary and triumphal arch is particularly valued for depicting 16C pilgrim attire so clearly.

Top *The calvary at
St-Thégonnec.*
Left *The calvary at Pleyben.*

GAZETTEER

Brasparts – 9km (6 miles) north of Pleyben
Situated at the heart of the Arrée Mountains
(Monts d'Arrée), this hill village has a 16C
parish close and an active craft centre, **La
Maison des Artisans**. There is a wide choice
of hiking and horse-riding trails from the
village. Gypsy-caravan tours explore the
isolated **Chapel of St-Michel de Brasparts**
and the great lake of the same name.

Kernascléden★★
– 30km (19 miles) west of Pontivy
The pride of this small village is
its 15C Gothic church, built by
the Rohan family. The stonework is extremely delicate, and
it is unusual in having two
porches; the south porch is
decorated with carvings of the
12 apostles. The interior frescoes
are remarkably well preserved.

Moncontour – 23km (14 miles)
south-east of St-Brieuc
Towered ramparts still partially
encircle this old town built at
the junction of two valleys.
Merchants' houses from the
town's prosperous days as a
centre of the linen industry line
narrow cobbled streets with
stone stairways and archways.
The town gateway – the postern
arch of St-Jean – survives from
the medieval era, with
remnants of the ramparts which
survived the demolition
ordered by Richelieu in 1626.

Ploërmel – 12km (8miles) east of Josselin
Although a settlement since the 6C, visitors
must search for traces of the past in this
thriving commercial and industrial town.
Ploërmel was once the seat of the dukes of
Brittany and the 16C **Church of St-Armel**
houses statues of these ancient Breton
dukes. **Maison des Marmousets** in Rue
Beaumanoir has a particularly fine façade.
Fractions of the 12C castle tower and
ramparts survive in Place Daversin.

Detail of figures
inside the lovely
church in
Kernascléden.

Ploërmel boasts an extensive leisure lake,
Duke's Pool (Étang au Duc), 2.5km (1.5
miles) north of the town, which includes its
own artificial beach and good watersports
facilities.

Quintin – 20km (12 miles) south-west of
St-Brieuc
Terraced streets around the **castle** spill down
to the river Gouët. Built on the edge of a
lake, this settlement consists of 17C and 18C
buildings. Old mills and dignified
merchants' houses survive from the days
when Quintin was a prosperous linen centre,
an era recalled in the local museum.

Redon – 58km (36 miles) south-east of
Josselin
Redon stands at the junction of the Nantes–
Brest Canal and the river Vilaine. Formerly a
commercial port, it is now a popular boating
centre; scenic stretches of the canal have
been preserved. Elegant 15C to 18C houses
have survived in the old town, and the Quay
Duguay-Trouin is lined with handsome ship-
owners' houses. The former abbey church of
St-Sauveur has a lovely Romanesque tower.

THE CHANNEL COAST

Stretches of the dramatic and varied coastline between Cancale and Morlaix have names such as the **Emerald Coast** (Côte d'Émeraude) and the **Pink Granite Coast** (Côte de Granit Rose) giving some clues to their beauty. Long-established as a holiday area, historic ports and traditional towns have been joined by new marinas and resorts, providing visitors with a wide choice.

Cancale to St-Brieuc

At **Cancale★** the flat St-Michel Bay finishes with a craggy flourish and the old town spills down in solid Victorian terraces to the 1 000ha (2 469 acres) spread of foreshore oyster beds, for which the town is renowned. Oysters are available from a host of restaurants, café-bars and stalls and there is even an **Oyster and Shellfish Museum** (Musée de l'Huître et du Coquillage).

There is a wide range of fresh seafood for sale at Cancale.

From the colourful working harbour a designated 4km (2½ mile) coast path winds to the headland of Grouin Point (Pointe du Grouin) through woods and wild flowers, revealing progressively grander seascapes across tothe Ile des Landes with its cormorant colony.

Westwards is **Rothéneuf Haven**, celebrated for its sandy beach and the strange **Sculptured Rocks** (Rochers sculptés) on the headland above – the work of a local priest in the 19C.

St-Malo★★★ is a thriving commercial

You can take one of these special boats to look at the oyster beds at Cancale.

The unusual Sculptured Rocks, set in the rugged headland, were carved by a local priest in the 19C.

69

fishing harbour, ferry port, seaside resort and historic walled city. One of the best ways to explore St-Malo is to walk round the formidable rampart walls, which in part date back to the 12C. Offshore, to the north, is the **National Fort** (Fort National), built by Vauban in 1689 to guard the city. Views from here include the islets of Grand Bé and Petit Bé; the tomb of writer Chateaubriand (1768–1848) lies on the former, which can be reached on foot at low tide.

At the north-east corner of the walls is the

There are bargains to be had in the bustling open-air market at St-Malo.

castle, now the town hall and **Museum of Local History and Ethnography** (Musée d'Histoire de la ville et d'Ethnographie du pays malouin). Towards the centre is **St-Vincent Cathedral** with its celebrated modern stained-glass windows. The social centre of the town – Place Jean-de-Chatillon and Place Chateaubriand – buzz with café life and haute-couture boutiques.

For the best views of St-Malo, walk along the **Aleth Coast Path** (Corniche d'Aleth) to **St-Servan-sur-Mer★**, just to the south of the city. Commanding the Rance estuary here is **Solidor Tower** (Tour Solidor), now housing the **International Museum of Cape Horn Vessels** (Musée International du Long Cours Cap-Hornier).

Across the Rance estuary lies **Dinard★★★**, which may not be so richly historic as St-Malo but its **Grand Beach** (Grande Plage) ranks among the best of up-market, smart-

Regimental changing tents line the prestigious Grand Beach, Dinard.

Boules is a popular pastime on the broad beaches.

set playgrounds where international high-rollers throng the casino. Stroll along the elegant Promenade du Clair de Lune with its views, flowers and Mediterranean atmosphere to see why Dinard is called the 'Gem of the Emerald Coast'.

In complete contrast is medieval **Dinan★★**, just 22km (14 miles) upriver from Dinard, full of history and a world apart. Here is a rich tapestry of Brittany's past: look for Place Du-Guesclin, where the Breton hero (*see* p.13) straddles his war-horse, sword half raised, perhaps in salute to his wife who was born here. Nearby, the mighty 14C **castle** boasts a unique oval-shaped keep and some 3km (2 miles) of 13C ramparts which keep the wide cordon of modern Dinan at bay. Within the old walls, the **Rue de l'Horloge** is just one of many fascinating, tortuous cobbled streets lined with huddles of half-timbered dwellings.

View of Old Dinan, with the Pont Gothique spanning the river.

Visitors to Dinan should not miss the **Pont Gothique**, best seen from the lofty viaduct road N176.

The **Fête des Remparts**, held every other year in September against an authentic backdrop, is a spectacular evocation of the Middle Ages: a pageant involving 5 000 participants and thousands more spectators.

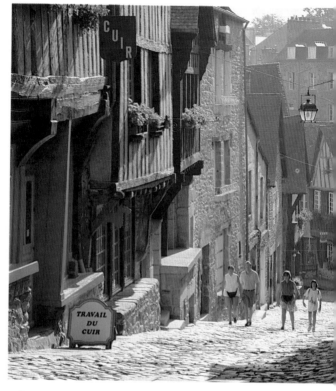

En route to the huge bay of **St-Brieuc** to the west there are more high spots. The bracing headland resorts of **St-Jacut-de-la-Mer★** and **St-Cast-le-Guildo★★** have their devotees, while **Cape Fréhel★★★** is worth visiting, not only for its natural splendour but for the nearby castle of **Fort-la-Latte★★**. This has endured in its hostile location since the 14C. On the GR34 trail, look for the neolithic menhir known as **Gargantua's Finger**.

There are some lovely timbered houses and cobbled streets to explore in Dinan.

Cape Fréhel is a dramatic and rugged stretch of coastline.

The Cape itself has 72m (236ft) high cliffs of sandstone and granite and is a haunt of seabirds which wheel above tiny offshore islands. This is one of the wildest stretches of Brittany's coastline.

Further round the bay is conifer-fringed **Pléhérel-Plage** and a wide swathe of sand dunes favoured by caravanners. **Sables-d'Or-les-Pins★** lives up to its name ('golden sands and pine trees'), the trees shading discreet

and sedate hotels. Rather more flamboyant
is nearby **Erquy★**, with its expanded marina:
a fast-growing family resort. There are good
walks around Cap d'Erquy. Footpaths circle
the headland knoll above **Le Val-André★★**,
which claim to be the best beach along the
north Brittany coast. Certainly the superfine
sands are inviting, backed by gracious and
dignified turn-of-the-century villas. The
esplanade here extends for more than 2km
(1 mile) and there are sailing schools at
either end, plus a new 18-hole links golf
course and a casino.

    St-Brieuc★, the Côtes d'Armor capital, is

*The harbour at
Erquy is backed
with cliffs topped
by pine trees.*

beautifully situated but it has also been industrialized. The old town centre is interesting though, with 14C **St-Stephen's Cathedral** (Cathédrale St-Étienne) which was powerfully fortified and thus able to survive many destructive attacks made on the port and town. Adjacent is a well-planned pedestrian precinct and a maze of colourful medieval streets, including Rue Fardel and Rue de Gouët, where James II of England lodged in 1689.

Not far from St-Brieuc's urban spread is the tiny port of **Binic★**, a delightful old-world fishing village that has escaped drastic

The quaint and unspoilt harbour at Binic is full of small boats.

development. The small-boat harbour is backed by traditional artisan houses, sandy beaches and low wooded hills, and there is the benefit of spacious car parking.

Nearby **St-Quay-Portrieux★** has been developed by the tourist industry as a popular family resort. It is also a watersports mecca, with no less than five safety-patrolled beaches. A new marina holds more than 1 000 pleasure craft.

By contrast, find **Plage Bonaparte,** north-west of Plouha, by turning off the D786 at Le Dernier Sou (the Last Farthing). Here, in 1944, under the noses of occupying Germans, 135 allied airmen were ferried in small boats back to England. This beach is still remote and secluded, much enjoyed now by cliff walkers and those seeking a quieter aspect of Brittany's coast.

Paimpol to Morlaix

The next place to make for is **Paimpol**, with its many and varied leisure attractions. Lively but not frenetic, and carefully commercialized, the town has a colourful harbour, a fine fish market in Place Gambetta, some elegant tree-shaded squares, and a miniature Latin Quarter. The **Maritime Museum** (Musée de la Mer) in Rue de la Benne recalls Paimpol's seafaring history from the days of cod-fishing in Newfoundland to the present.

The pedestrian-only **Bréhat Island★★** with its bird sanctuary is just a ten-minute ferry ride offshore from Arcouest Point (Pointe de l'Arcouest), 5km (3 miles) north of Paimpol. South-east is the atmospheric 13C ruin of **Beauport Abbey★** (Abbaye de Beauport).

Other interesting local excursions from Paimpol include **Loguivy-de-la-Mer**, a

Beauport Abbey, an evocative 13C ruin, has a delightful foreshore setting at Kerity, near Paimpol.

traditional lobster-fishing village on a little-visited headland to the north which has been bypassed by the 20C, and the **Talbert Spit** (Sillon de Talbert) on the west bank of the Trieux estuary. This narrow shingle causeway points seawards for 2km (1 mile) and is walkable at low water.

In total contrast is the moon-scape foreshore around **Plougrescant**, where the famous **House in the Chasm** (privately-owned) is squashed impossibly between granite slabs near the recognized gateway to the Pink Granite Coast, **Tréguier★★**. Two rivers (Jaudy and Guindy) form a half-moon around this once-fortified port and former capital of the ancient Trégor province. There are many picturesque corners here, with old corn lofts along Rue Ernest Renan, an ancient bishop's palace, and twin towers flanking the quayside town gate. Towering **St-Tugdual Cathedral** (Cathédrale St-Tugdual) holds the tomb of St Yves, patron saint of lawyers. The vast interior is stunning.

EXPLORING BRITTANY

Inland, behind the craggy coastline between Tréguier and the queen of Channel Coast resorts, **Perros-Guirec★★**, is a gorse-covered plateaux bisected by farm lanes. At Perros-Guirec the granite is tinged with a hundred different shades of pink, lending colour to this popular resort, with its superb sandy beaches.

Ploumanach Beach★★, which can be reached from Perros-Guirec via a three-hour cliff path, has some of the best of these strange rose-pink rocks, as does nearby

Rose-pink granite boulders and wide open vistas are typical of this stretch of coast, such as here at Ploumanach.

Trégastel Plage★★, where giant boulders are individually named according to theirshape: Napoleon's Hat, the Gnome, the Tortoise, etc. So wide and spacious is this stretch of coast that even at the height of the season it is seldom overcrowded.

For those who fancy even quieter waters, however, there is nearby **Trébeurden★**, along with Ile-Grande which is linked by a causeway. Megalithic remains can be found here, and there is also a hospital for seabirds.

Inland lies the wet-weather attraction of **Trégor Planetarium** (Planétarium du Trégor). Nearby is the **Radar Dome and Telecommunications Museum** (Radôme et musée des Télécommunications), a fascinating exhibition tracing the development of communication technology over the last 150 years.

For a glimpse of Man's earlier history visit **Barnenez Tumulus★** (Cairn de Barnenez), a 6 000-year-old burial chamber just north of Morlaix on the Kernéléhen Peninsula.

Further along the coast is the picturesque port of **Morlaix★**. Initially fortified by the Romans, it was often attacked, most memorably in 1522 when an English fleet of 60 ships invaded the bay. To prevent a similar invasion a fortress was built at the estuary entrance – **Bull's Castle** (Château du Taureau) – and it still stands guard to this day.

The medieval town of Morlaix is dominated by a towering **viaduct** (viaduc) which carries the main Paris to Brest railway line. In its shadow lies the **Church of St-Mélaine**, with its delicate 15C stonework, and **Queen Anne's House** (Maison de la Reine Anne) in Rue du Mur, a three-storey building embellished with statues of saints and grotesques.

Morlaix's heart is in and around **Place des Otages**, where the atmosphere is restful, the pace of life easy, and the pavement cafés pleasantly busy.

The sandy beaches at Trégastel are littered with huge boulders, many individually named.

GAZETTEER

Bréhat Island★★

Consisting of two islets linked by an 18C bridge, Bréhat lies just offshore of Paimpol. Cars are not allowed here (there is a 1 000-vehicle car park at Paimpol's ferry port), so tractors transport visitors.

The little township, **Le Bourg**, has a church with 12C remnants, but the main attractions of the island are its mild climate – fig trees and mimosa flourish and there is always a profusion of flowers – its rocky inlets and reefs and its rich birdlife.

Carantec★ – 15km (9 miles) north-west of Morlaix

On a headland jutting into Morlaix Bay, this resort is conveniently close to Morlaix and St-Pol-de-Léon (*see* pp.82 and 86); despite this, it is relatively uncrowded. There are some attractive sandy beaches, coupled with a number of way-marked woodland walks between cliffs, and the **Priest's Chair** (La Chaise du Curé) is a noted viewpoint.

Guingamp – 30km (19 miles) west of St-Brieuc

Located between the Armor and the Argoat this one-time market town is now largely commercial. The old heart survives around **Place du Centre** and the **Hôtel de Ville** is housed in an old Knights Templar monastery. In 1343, Edward III of England stormed the town and held it for a year.

Jugon-les-Lacs – 22km (14 miles) west of Dinan

Two rivers form the beautiful 67ha (166 acre) Lake Jugon, which has lakeside walks and watersports. The village itself clusters around a 13C church, and there is a pretty old manor house off Place Centrale.

Lamballe – 18 km (11 miles) south-east of St-Brieuc

It is as the home of the **national stud** (*haras national*) that Lamballe, a lively but unremarkable hill town, is best known. Here every breed in the equine world is bred. Tours include the stables, smithy, carriage house, harness room and riding school.

Lannion★ – 10km (6 miles) south of Perros-Guirec

Lannion is a good base for touring the Pink Granite Coast and it also has one of the best shopping centres in the area. Founded in the 11C, there are only a few reminders of the past in this split-level river port. It is now a telecommunications centre. Some medieval half-timbered houses are preserved around **Place du Général Leclerc**. **Brélévenez Church** was built on a hill by the Knights Templar in the 12C.

St-Briac-sur-Mer★ – 8km (5 miles) west of Dinard

A photogenic fishing harbour and wide sandy beaches are features of this pretty resort west of Dinard. It is also famous for its annual Seagull Festival in August.

St-Jean-du-Doigt★ – west of Lannion

The little church here is said to hold the severed finger of St John the Baptist, a relic returned from the Holy Land in the 15C – hence the village's name. It lies on a tranquil stretch of coast, just inland from a fine sandy beach.

FINISTÈRE

For centuries this westerly *département* of Brittany has both battled with the sea and looked to it for its livelihood. Finistère is also a stronghold of the Breton culture – language, costume and tradition – and heartland of the unique parish closes.

Roscoff to St-Mathieu Point

Roscoff★, a popular seaside resort, ferry port and fishing port for lobster, is also known as a medical centre, the birthplace of *thalassothérapie* (sea-water therapy). Attractions for the visitor include the **Roch-Hievec Tropical Gardens** (Jardin exotique de Roch-Hievec) and the **Charles Pérez Aquarium**.

Offshore, **Batz Island** (Ile de Batz), a 20-minute ferry ride away from the port, is an established sailing centre.

Nearby **St-Pol-de-Léon★** has a market-town atmosphere and good visitor facilities, plus a nice bathing beach at Pempoul, adjacent to Kernevez park. It also boasts two fine buildings, the former **cathedral** (Ancienne Cathédrale) and the 14C **Kreisker Chapel** (Chapelle du Kreisker) with its distinctive belfry.

The appeal of this area is its tranquillity and relative seclusion. Horse-riding and cycling are popular pursuits. Away from the rugged coast, the region is still largely a market-garden centre, as it has been for centuries.

Much of the north-west coast, known as the **Côte des Abers★** (*abers* are shallow estuaries into which small streams flow) is uncrowded, becoming wilder to the west of the Aber-Wrac'h and Aber-Benoît estuaries, which bite into the gorse-carpeted slopes. The population is thin around France's most westerly headland, Corsen Point (Pointe de Corsen), a 50m (160ft) cliff.

Offshore lies lonely **Ile Molène** and more distant still is **Ushant★★** (Ile d'Ouessant), now a recognized resort serviced not only by ferry but also by air from Brest.

Just down the coast is **Le Conquet★**, a fishing harbour of charm and character nestling in a snug haven; very different from the nearby **St-Mathieu Point★★**. This headland, towering over a rock-strewn

*colourful corner
[i]n peaceful and
[u]nspoilt Le
[C]onquet.*

The remains of a 6C Benedictine Monastery at St-Mathieu Point was reputed to have had the head of St Matthew as its holy relic.

channel, is crowned by a 6C cliff-top abbey ruin, a monument to lost sailors, and a modern lighthouse (*phare*).

Brest to Quimper

Inland and south-east of Brest (*see* p.98), an interesting rural route via Landerneau, La Roche-Maurice and Sizun leads to the **Armorique Regional Nature Park**. A busy market town on the Elorn estuary, **Landerneau** is the old capital of Léon province. Spanning the river is the **Rohan Bridge** (Pont de Rohan), which supports two rows of houses with overhanging upper storeys. It is one of the last inhabited bridges in Europe. The **Church of St Thomas of Canterbury** has a triple-tiered steeple, and there is a former ossuary next door.

La Roche-Maurice★ is a hill village below the gaunt but impressive remains of a medieval castle. It also has a celebrated parish close (*see* pp.64-65) where the 17C ossuary inscription warns that 'Death Comes to All'.

Sizun★, even smaller, displays a miniature Roman triumphal arch. Authentically dressed Breton peasant models can be seen in the chapel museum.

South of here, in an appropriately pastoral setting, the **Maison du Parc** is an interesting and informative visitor centre at the western end of the Arrée Mountains (Monts d'Arrée). Many visitors set off from here on a circuit drive of the **Crozon Peninsula★★★** (Presqu'île de Crozon), where

The triple triumphal arch of the Sizun parish close dates from 1585–1588.

the seascape views from Dinan Point (Pointe de Dinan) and Cape Chèvre (Cap de la Chèvre) are magnificent. Small sandy beaches nestle between sandstone and quartz cliffs, and there is potential for sailing, horse-riding and cliff-walking around Morgat, just north of Cape Chèvre.

Crozon itself is unattractive but practical, with a wide choice of accommodation and cycle-hire facilities. It is much used by caravanners who congregate in this vicinity.

Camaret-sur-Mer, Brittany's most westerly seaside town, has considerable character and is a good base for exploring the area. The old part of the town is at the foot of a steep hill, close to the commercial fishing harbour

The far-reaching views from Ménez-Hom are well worth the climb.

which is France's principal source of lobster.

There are some invigorating headland walks above the town. Here also are the **Lagatjar Alignments** (Alignements de Lagatjar), a group of nearly 150 menhirs discovered this century. On Sillon Point (Pointe de Sillon) there is a tower by Vauban (**Château Vauban**) which survives as a powerful landmark from the 17C, along with a fascinating chapel of the same period, **Notre-Dame-de-Rocamadour**, originally a 12C pilgrimage chapel.

Turning inland, there is another landmark which has long been a place of pilgrimage, the isolated dome of Brittany's highest pinnacle, **Ménez-Hom**

he chapel of t-Marie du Ménez- Iom has a simple ut eyecatching alvary.

(330m/1 082ft). The ascent to the summit is rewarded with sweeping views westwards. Since earliest times Ménez-Hom has been a place of worship, both pagan and Christian, and a festival is still held here in mid-summer – nowadays a great Breton clan gathering.

Between Ménez-Hom and Crozon, the village of **Argol** is worth a detour. Here there is a traditional Breton craft centre where ancient trades such as clog-making, open-fire forging, butter-churning, charcoal-making and other traditional skills are

The small town of Locronan has a large 15C church, St-Ronan, which is linked to Le Penity Chapel.

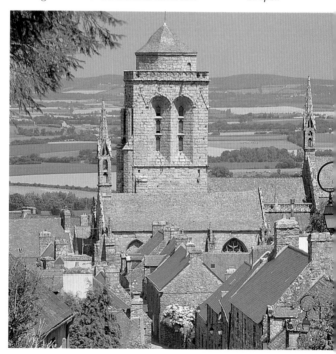

demonstrated by experts.

South of Ménez-Hom is medieval **Locronan****, a delightful rural village that has survived the march of time. The granite and slate-roof houses of the main street are dominated by the 15C **Church of St-Ronan** and **Le Penity Chapel** (Église St-Ronan et chapelle du Penity). Planned like a scaled-down cathedral, the interior of this four-square church is strikingly atmospheric. It stands in Grande Place, a cobbled expanse surrounded by a riotous tumble of steep-pitched roofs, capped dormer windows and ancient arches.

Visitors pay a modest car-parking and entry fee to wander around this living museum-piece of Finistère. It is also the assembly point for countless *pardon* processions (known here as *Troménies*), to Chapelle Plach-Ar, some 2km (1 mile) above the village on a hill called **The Troménies**.

Further south, an even richer feast of Breton history awaits visitors at **Quimper****. Standing by the Odet river, it resides in a steep-sided valley, making for a scenic approach. Park by the Steir (a tributary of the Odet), where there is room for 1 000 cars, and walk along the Rue du Parc. Off here, in Place St-Corentin, is the great cathedral of the same name. This is a granite masterpiece of Gothic intricacy and stained glass, with parts dating from the mid-13C. The building is laimed to be the most glorious place of worship in western France. The soaring twin towers are actually 19C restorations – tributes to modern stone-masons. Legendary King Gradlon gazes down from between the towers. He lost his original city of Ys, in the kingdom of Cornouaille, beneath the waves in the 6C,

and adopted Quimper instead, guarding its
fortunes ever since.

To the north of the cathedral is the **Fine
Arts Museum** (Musée des Beaux-Arts)
housed in a modern building behind a 19C
façade. From here wander in any direction
to absorb the atmosphere of Breton city life.
The place names sometimes indicate earlier
industry. Place au Beurre, once cluttered
with earthenware jars of salted butter, is
evocative alongside attractive modern
pedestrian precincts and shops, including a
spacious covered fruit and vegetable market.

*There is a square
kilometre of
medieval streets
and alleys to
explore in Quimper*

For more of old Quimper see Quai du
Steir and Rue Élie-Fréron where some of the
houses date back to the Middle Ages; and
the **Hotel de Ville** with paintings by Rubens,
Vélesquez and Picasso. The **Folk Museum**
(Musée Départemental Breton), in Rue de
Roi Gradlon, displays exhibits ranging from
Gallo-Roman relics to 16C regional costume
and, of course, glazed earthenware – *faïence*
– in this the ceramic-ware capital of Brittany.
The **Faïence Museum** (Musée de la faïence)
in Rue J B Bousquet traces over 300 years of
Quimper's pottery making. About 2 500

*vidence of the
amous Quimper
aïence is all
round the town –
ere used with
lowers to decorate
shop front.*

items are displayed and the craft is explained.

Yet more medieval architecture is evident in Place Terre-au-Duc and along Rue Kéréon, rich in half-timbered façades and overhanging jetties.

Both to the north and south of Quimper the coast is attractive. **Pont-l'Abbé**, some 18km (11 miles) south, is an old trading port prettily sited on the Pont-l'Abbé river and protected by a 14C castle. Housed in the castle keep is the **Bigouden Museum** (Musée Bigouden) with collections of costumes, lace head-dresses (*coiffes*) and furniture and fishing paraphernalia. There is a medieval monastery chapel and church ruin near the quay. A leisure park has been created round the barrage lake.

Between the fishing harbour of **Loctudy** and **Eckmühl Lighthouse★** (Phare d'Eckmühl) a series of sand and shingle beaches is backed by marshy estuaries. This is lonely terrain, and the **Notre-Dame-de-Tronoën Calvary and Chapel★★**, north of Penmarch Point (Pointe de Penmarch), is quite isolated. The calvary is claimed to be the oldest in Brittany.

On the northern shore of vast Audierne Bay (Baie d'Audierne), straddling the wide waters of the Goyen estuary, is **Audierne** port, famous for its shellfish. This is a popular family resort with good amenities and some natural highlights. The bathing beach near the bustling harbour – where a ferry goes to tiny **Sein Island** (Ile de Sein) 12km (7½ miles) distant – is one of the best in south Finistère, especially renowned for its clear-water skin-diving.

Visit **Raz Point★★★** (Pointe du Raz) and the **Trépassés Bay** (Baie des Trépassés) – Bay of the Dead – when the surf is crashing and

A walk around Raz Point is always spectacular – especially in stormy weather – but the cliff walk is not for those nervous of heights.

the spume flying. This rocky spur defying the Atlantic is breathtaking, particularly in the early morning before the huge car park is filled. Explore the cliff path with caution, particularly around **Hell's Mouth Chasm** (Enfer de Plogoff), where a fearful tidal-race sweeps 70m (230ft) below.

The sands, reached by a steeply descending road, are seemingly infinite. Here deceased Druids were laid, before being ferried to Sein Island for burial. Thankfully the bay remains almost totally undeveloped, and hauntingly beautiful.

GAZETTEER

Armorique Regional Nature Park
Created in 1969, this includes 112 000ha (276 750 acres) of western Brittany, as well as offshore islands, such as Ushant, the Arrée Mountains and the Aulne estuary. The park's main aims are to preserve the countryside and encourage local industry.

Brest★
Brest was developed as a great naval base in the 16C, and today its shipyards build the largest ships in France. During the Second World War, the historic harbour and old town were almost totally destroyed. The modern city is laid out in a grid pattern with wide avenues and open spaces. All that remains of the past is the **castle**, now housing the **Maritime Museum** (Musée de la Marine), and the **Tanguy Tower** (Tour Tanguy) opposite. Built in the 14C, this now houses the **Museum of Old Brest**. East of the commercial port is the **Océanopolis**, a centre for the study of marine life with numerous displays and exhibitions.

Châteaulin – 30km (19 miles) north of Quimper
A popular base for the Armorique Regional Nature Park, this sedate old town straddles the river Aulne. Between steep and wooded hills, it provides excellent seasonal salmon fishing and horse-riding. Other good sporting facilities include five tennis courts and a heated indoor pool.

Daoulas★ – 24km (15 miles) south-east of Brest
Beside the Daoulas river there is a 12C abbey

with an atmospheric cloister ruin, and a 16C parish close with a host of carved figures. To the east, the **Plougastel Peninsula** (Presqu'île de Plougastel) is a fruit-growing centre.

Douarnenez★ – 23km (14 miles) north-west of Quimper

With a long history of sardine and lobster fishing, Douarnenez has evolved as one of France's high-ranking commercial fishing ports, while maintaining much local trade as well. The **Port Museum** (Port-Musée) consists of a boat museum with craft from all over Europe, a floating museum, and shipyard and repair workshops which together provide all the information you could want on maritime history. Beaches, watersports and good walking country add to the appeal of the town as a resort.

Le Folgoët★★ – 23km (14 miles) north-east of Brest

Although this ancient parish has been absorbed into Lesneven, it is still a pilgrim shrine for one of Brittany's greatest annual *pardons*. The 15C Gothic **Notre-Dame Basilica's** interior is very impressive, with a fine granite rood screen. The old district of Folgoët is suffused with Breton legend; the name translates as 'Fool in the Woods'.

Kerjean Castle★ – 5km (3 miles) south-west of Plouzévédé

Kerjean, built around 1550, was called by Louis XIII 'one of the handsomest of homes in my Kingdom'. It is the centre-piece of a regal, 800ha (1 977 acre) park – a state-owned, partly-restored ruin rich in Renaissance treasures.

ENJOYING YOUR VISIT

Weather

Brittany basks in a temperate climate similar – though less quickly changeable – to that of the British Isles. The far western peninsula has the highest average rainfall, while the eastern areas enjoy the drier, less windy weather systems of Europe's land-mass. The mean annual sunshine total of 2 000 hours is equal to that of southern France, although the temperature is more moderate at a comfortable 64°F (18°C).

Sea breezes strengthen, sometimes considerably, west of Pontivy, but the Gulf stream ensures that prevailing westerlies do not bite too sharply, even in winter.

Luck is needed for any holiday, but generally mid-May to September are the best months to visit Brittany. Early October, however, is often stable and golden; ideal for coastal or country exploration.

Traditional Breton costume is usually an essential element of festivals

Entertainment

During the summer months colourful entertainment of all kinds – dancing, concerts, art exhibitions, theatre – takes place at the numerous summer fêtes and festivals held all over Brittany (*see* pp. 101-103). West of Pontivy, especially in country areas, the Breton *fest-noz* (night feasts) are the traditional Celtic celebration of annual events such as harvestime, nowadays a blend of old-time *paysan* music and dance, coupled with orthodox partying. Visitors are always welcomed at these evening celebrations.

Most of the resort **casinos** are found on the north coast and these establishments are now increasingly ready to accept casual dress and include bars and discos, which in turn proliferate in most towns.

There are a few *son-et-lumière* shows which are popular with locals and visitors alike. Some are beautifully produced and of high technical merit, such as the *Tristan and Isolde* spectacular at Elven Towers (*see* p.53).

Calendar of Events

Bretons are past-masters at combining religious homage with secular fun, so that whatever the celebration – in a small village or major city – everyone has a good time, no matter how solemn the event, be it a *pardon* (*see* pp.20-21) or sea blessing. Some of the most important events are listed here; the dates are variable in many cases.

La Baule: Concours d'Élegance Automobile. Summer car festival held near the harbour annually since 1924. July or August.

Belle-Île: Breton games with all the trimmings, including wrestling bouts. 3rd Sunday in August.

Brière Nature Park: Traditional marsh-dwellers gathering and barge race (Fédrun). Mid-August.

Camaret-sur-Mer: *Pardon* of Notre-Dame de Rocamadour and Blessing of the Sea. 1st Sunday in September.

Carnac: Festival of the Menhir Alignements; one of the most ancient of Breton ceremonies. 3rd Sunday in August.

Concarneau: Celebrated Finistère event, Festival of Blue Nets (Fêtes des Filets Bleus). 2nd week in August.

Dinan: La Fête des Remparts. Medieval spectacular beneath feudal castle walls. Last weekend in August or beginning of September, every other year.

Dinard: Firework displays and evening Spectacle d'Ambience along Moonlight Promenade (Promenade du Clair de Lune). Throughout July and August.

Folgoët: North Finistère's *Grand Pardon* procession which manages to last for two days! 1st or 2nd Sunday in September.

Guingamp: Week-long Breton dance festival; music ancient and modern. August.

Lorient: Inter-Celtic Festival. Celts gather from all over Europe for traditional feasting, dancing and music-making. 1st and 2nd week in August.

Nantes: Carnival weekend, a colourful French/Breton blend celebrating historic carnival and thanksgiving. Eve of Easter.
Paimpol: Icelandic and Newfoundland Festival, celebrating maritime discoveries of old. 4th Sunday in August.
Paimpont: Festival de Brocéliande. Homage to King Arthur and Knights of the Round Table is paid at this picturesque forest village. 2nd week in June.
Perros-Guirec: Pilgrimage of Notre-Dame de la Clarté (3km/2 miles west of town). Night procession and hill-top bonfire. Mid-August.
Pont-Aven: Festival of Golden Gorse (Fêtes des fleurs d'Ajoncs) and *pardon*. 1st Sunday in August.
Quimper: The annual religious and secular gathering of the ancient Cornouaille region. 3rd week in July.
Ste-Anne-d'Auray: The famous *Grand Pardon* de Sainte-Anne procession. 25 and 26 July.
Vannes: Festival of Arvor, 15 August. Medieval midsummer fête – Morbihan's most spectacular. Second weekend in July.

Food and Drink
Fish and **seafood** is one of the great attractions of Brittany. Harbour-side cafés and restaurants at Cancale, Concarneau and countless other places along the coast serve a wondrous variety of fish. Mackerel, bass, mullet, sea-bream, hake and sardines compete with mussels (*moules*) lobster (*homard*), crab and oysters (*huîtres*); of the latter, Belon oysters are said to be the best in the world. No one should leave Brittany without having sampled a *plateau de fruits de mer,* a huge, colourful plate of seafood of all kinds. Alternatively, try *cotriade*, a sort of Breton *bouillabaisse*.

créperies serve these famous Breton specialities all through the day.

For the rest, the Breton diet relies on traditional dishes using first-class ingredients. These include salt-pasture lamb (*prés-salés*), lamb and haricot beans (*gigot à la Bretonne*), chicken cooked in cider and served with apples (*poulet au cidre*) and locally raised duck (*canard*), turkey (*dinde*), guinea fowl (*pintade*) and pork dishes. Excellent fresh **vegetables** are available all year, and these include beans, leeks, onions, asparagus and artichokes.

Crêpes are another speciality of Brittany. Made to order, they are available at any time of day and served with a range of fillings from ham and mussels to syrup and ice cream. *Galettes*, made with buckwheat flour, are the savoury variety, whereas *crêpes*, made with wheat flour, have sweet fillings.

Other **sweet specialities** include the Breton *quatre-quarts* pound cake, a 46cm (18 inch) long butter-filled treat also found in every supermarket, and *far Breton*, a flan often filled with prunes or raisins.

Brittany is not known for its own **cheeses**, but a good selection from all over France is usually available, particularly from neighbouring Normandy.

Cider is Brittany's traditional drink, fermented mainly around Fouesnant. It comes in a variety of forms and is also used widely in cooking. Some brews are surprisingly potent.

The local **wine** is Muscadet and its variants, produced along the western banks of the Loire; at its best it is a magnificent white wine,Always look for the Muscadet-sur-Lie (sediment-aged). Chilled, this is the perfect partner to fish or white meat dishes and a splendid *aperitif.* You can also get Grosplant from the Nantes coastal region.

Shopping

In general, the French tend to be exacting shoppers and the major towns in Brittany have fashionable international shopping centres which satisfy this demand for high quality.

If you are looking for good Breton souvenirs, however, try and buy from their place of origin: Quimper for fine **ceramics**, Batz or Dol-de-Bretagne for genuine *sabots*, Lannion for **hand-made furniture**, the Brière region for **wickerwork**, Pont l'Abbé for **lace**, St-Malo, Fourgères and Vitré for **copper** and **metal-ware**. For **religious souvenirs** visit the parish close villages; for **carved granite**, Carnac – or Perros-Guirec if you prefer the stone pink-tinted.

Brittany has its share of craftsmen, such as this wood carver, producing traditional gifts and souvenirs.

For **Breton antiques** the flea-markets of La Baule, Vannes, Nantes, Morlaix, etc, sometimes offer high quality, occasionally low-priced, artefacts.

Most sizeable towns (and many small ones) have peripheral **hypermarkets** (*hypermarchés*) selling a tremendous range of goods – from food to garden equipment – at the keenest prices, with generous parking.

Supermarkets (*supermarchés*) are smaller and generally sell only food. They have been in existence longer than hypermarkets and are usually nearer the town centre.

One very enjoyable aspect of shopping in Brittany is the **outdoor market**. Usually taking place weekly (sometimes twice) in the mornings, it is an intrinsic part of Breton life and the ideal place to buy cheese, fruit, meat, flowers, trinkets, household items and much more.

Dinghies setting off for a sail at La Baule.

Sport

Brittany's topography and climate allows ramblers, hikers, cyclists and joggers to exercise vigorously without risk of dehydration or – using normal precautions – savage sunburn. Inland hills may only rise to around 300m (985ft), but in context they are challenging enough to be stimulating. A good network of marked paths cover the region and numerous guides are sold locally in bookshops and tourist offices. *Sentiers de grande randonnée* (GR on maps) criss-cross the region, and *sentiers de petit randonnée* (PR on maps) are circular routes up to about 25km (16 miles) long.

Brittany has few peers for **watersports**. The water is clean, and the choice is endless. Brittany is rated as one of the best cruising areas for offshore **yachting** in Europe, while

safe yet exciting **wind-surfing** is practised in
sheltered bays and gulfs such as Morbihan.

There are more than 600km (375 miles)
of inland waterways to explore, too, on the
Nantes–Brest canal and along reaches of the
Aulne and Blavet rivers, using a variety of
craft from canoes to multi-berth hire boats.

Scenic voyages are available all around the
coast, and you can board a sight-seeing
vedette as easily as you can hop on a ferry to
an offshore island.

Other sports facilities include a good
spread of **golf courses**, some right by the sea,
numerous public **tennis courts**, even in quite
small resorts and towns, and several **riding
centres** offering day treks or holidays.

THE BASICS

Before You Go

Visitors entering France should have a full passport, valid to cover the period in which they will be travelling. No visa is required for members of EU countries or US and Candian citizens, but visitors from Australia and New Zealand require an entry visa. This can be readily obtained from the French Embassies and Consulates in the home country. No vaccinations are necessary.

Getting There

Getting to France has never been easier, and now that Le Shuttle and Eurostar are officially up and running the choice is even wider for UK travellers.

Flights leave from all over the world for various destinations in France, including the two airports in Paris – Orly and Roissy-Charles de Gaulle – and are organized by both schedule and charter airlines.

Trains connect Paris with the airports and with several towns in Brittany. Eurostar runs from London via the Channel Tunnel to France in 3 hours, and Le Shuttle from Folkestone to Calais in about half an hour.

Several ferry companies carry cars and passengers across the Channel, with the quickest journey being between Dover/Calais. The hovercraft is even faster, crossing from Dover to Calais in just 35 minutes. Brittany Ferries offer crossings from Portsmouth and Plymouth directly to Brittany, docking at St Malo and Roscoff. For 24-hour road information ☎ 48 94 33 33.

An efficient railway service makes the connection between the ports and various towns throughout Brittany, and there are high-speed trains (TGV) to France from many European cities. There are also coach services throughout Europe, as well as between London and many destinations in France. If you plan to travel in the peak summer holiday period, be sure to book well in advance.

Arriving

There is no limit on the importation into France of tax-paid goods bought in an EU country provided they are for personal consumption, with the exception of alcohol and tobacco which have fixed limits governing them. Holidaymakers bringing a caravan into France for a period of less than six months are not governed by customs formalities.

The Tourist Information Office in Rue de l'Horloge, Dinan.

A-Z

Accidents and Breakdowns

Fully comprehensive insurance is advisable for motorists in France, and motoring organizations recommend that you carry a green card, although this is no longer a legal requirement. A red warning triangle must be carried by cars towing a caravan or a trailer, in case of breakdown. While this is not compulsory for non-towing cars with hazard warning lights, it is strongly recommended.

On autoroutes there are orange emergency telephones every 2km (1¼ miles), and assistance is charged at a Government-fixed rate. Motorists can only call the police or the official breakdown service operating in that area, and not their own breakdown company. This also applies on the Paris *périphérique*.

Check with your insurance company before leaving for France what you should do in case of an accident. Generally, if an accident happens and

nobody is hurt, a form *Constat à l'Amiable* should be completed with full details. This must be signed by both parties, and sent off to the relevant insurers. Where someone is injured in a road accident, contact the Ambulance Service (*Samu*) on ☎ 15. The Fire Brigade is on ☎ 18 and the Police on ☎ 17.

Accommodation

The *Michelin Red Guide France* lists a selection of hotels, while the *Places To Stay Map* in the *Green Guide Brittany* indicates recommended places for overnight stops. Brittany is ideally suited to holidaymakers seeking self-catering accommodation and good-quality camp sites as well as hotel and bed and breakfast rooms. The area has many fine seaside resorts, and inland towns and regions which are well worth a visit.

Staying in rural *gîtes* is a popular self-catering experience in the west of France, and details of over 2 000 such prop

rties can be obtained from:
Maison des Gîtes de France, 35
Rue Godot-de-Mauroy, 75009
Paris. ☎ 01 49 70 75 75

Bed and breakfast accommodation is also available in
France, and comes under the
name of Chambres d'hôtes –
there are literally hundreds of
these around the country.

Holders of an International
Youth Hostel Federation card
can get a list of French youth
hostels from: La Ligue Française
pour les Auberges de la
Jeunesse, 38 Boulevard Raspail,
75007 Paris. ☎ 01 45 48 69 84

Information on all of the
above accommodation can be
obtained from the French Government Tourist Office in your

own country (*see* **Tourist Information Offices** for addresses).

Airports *see* **Arriving p.108**

Babysitters *see* **Children**

Banks
Banks are open from 9am–
noon and 2–4pm on weekdays,
and are closed on Mondays or
Saturdays. They close at noon
on the day before a bank
holiday.

Banks exchange travellers'
cheques, and most also have
cash dispensers which accept
international credit cards. A
passport is necessary when
cashing cheques in a bank.
Some banks, but not all, will

*Visitors prepared to
explore off the
beaten track will
find delights such as
this rural cottage at
Lehon.*

change foreign money.
See also **Money**

Beaches

The jagged coastline of Brittany is liberally sprinkled with clean, sandy beaches, some spreading as far as the eye can see, and others small and pretty. The larger beaches often have organized, supervized play centres which children can join for a fee, and these may also offer windsurfing instruction and the hire of sail boards and boats. Ice cream, cold drinks and doughnut vendors parade up and down the beaches calling out their wares.

Bicycles

These can be hired from about 20 main railway stations throughout the region, and may be returned to a different station at the end of the rental period. Tourist information offices provide lists of places that hire bikes, and further details of cycling in Brittany are available from: Fédération Française de Cyclotourisme, 8 Rue Jean-Marie-Jégo, 75013 Paris. ☎ 01 45 80 30 21

Cyclists may also want to bring their own bicycles to Brittany, and the ferries and many trains will carry them free.

Books

Here are a few suggestions for reading to enhance your stay in Brittany.

The best account of the Arthurian legend is still Tennyson's *Idylls of the King*; children will like *The Once and Future King*, by T.H. White. The macabre story of a real-life knight is recounted by Leonard Wolf in *Bluebeard, the Life and Crimes and Gilles de Rais*, or novelized by E. Lucie-Smith in *The Dark Pageant*. Jules Verne's science fiction novels are still worth reading, and the *Letters of Abelard and Heloise* is a touching literary classic. There are several good general books on the Celts.

Breakdowns see Accidents

Buses see Transport

Camping

The French are very keen campers, and the country has many efficiently run sites offering a whole range of facilities. Some campsites offer fully-equipped and permanently sited mobile homes and family-sized tents. Details of these can usually be obtained through a travel agent or specialist company.

Touring sites are very professionally organized, and you

can choose from simple, basic sites in rural areas to large complexes with swimming pools, restaurants and entertainment. For full details of French sites see *Michelin Camping Caravaning France* or apply to Féderation Française de Camping et de Caravaning, 78 Rue de Rivoli, 75004 Paris. ☎ 01 42 72 84 08

Canal Trips *see* **Excursions**

Car Hire
Brittany is well stocked with

Walkers in Huelgoat Forest.

car-hire agencies, and there are outlets at airports, air terminals and railway stations as well as in all large towns. Airlines and tour operators offer fly/drive arrangements, and car hire in conjunction with train travel is one of the services available from French Railways.

Weekly rates with unlimited mileage offer the best deal; these include collision damage waiver, personal accident insurance and local tax, and can be booked from any country. The minimum age limit is 18, but few international companies hire to drivers under 20–23.

Drivers must have held their full licence for at least a year, and an international driving licence is required for non-EU nationals. With the exception of Avis, the maximum age limit is 60–65. Unless paying by credit card a substantial cash deposit is required, but full details of the different hire schemes can be obtained from tourist offices. *See also* **Accidents and Breakdowns**, and **Tourist Information Offices**

Children

Brittany is a children's paradise, with miles of safe clean beaches for paddling, swimming and playing in the sand. When the strong tides retreat, there are rockpools for exploring and crabbing. There are also fine aquariums at Dinard, Brest, St-Malo, Vannes, Le Croisic and Roscoff, plus special interest wildlife parks, bird reserves and treats like Malansac with its pre-history tableaux. Resorts developed expressly with the family in mind (among others) are St-Brévin-les-Pins, Trébeurden and, above all, Perros-Guirec. There are zoos at Pont-Scorff, Branféré and Trégomeur.

Restaurants in France, and especially in the holiday resorts along the west coast, welcome children and are completely tolerant of less-than-perfect table manners.

Disposable nappies, baby milk products and convenience baby foods are readily available everywhere.

Churches *see* Religion

Climate *see page 100*

Clothing

Comfortable casual clothing is ideal when holidaying in Brittany, with the emphasis on beachwear for days by the coast. More formal dress may be expected at some restau-

A timbered hotel in Dinan.

rants and casinos. Spring and autumn evenings can be chilly even on the warmest days, and an extra sweater or jacket is recommended. Even summer days can be quite cold and windy, when trousers, sweaters and warm jackets will be appreciated.

Most French clothing measurements are standard throughout Europe but differ from those in the UK and the US. The following are examples:

Dress Sizes

UK	8	10	12	14	16	18
France	36	38	40	42	44	46
US	6	8	10	12	14	16

Men's Suits

UK/US	36	38	40	42	44	46
France	46	48	50	52	54	56

Men's Shirts

UK/US	14	14.5	15	15.5	16	16.5	17
France	36	37	38	39/40	41	42	43

Men's Shoes

UK	7	7.5	8.5	9.5	10.5	11
France	41	42	43	44	45	46
US	8	8.5	9.5	10.5	11.5	12

Women's Shoes

UK	4.5	5	5.5	6	6.5	7
France	37	38	38	39	39	40
US	6	6.5	7	7.5	8	8.5

Consulates

Embassies and consulates can be found at the following addresses:

American Consulate 2 Rue St-Florentin, 75008 Paris.
☎ 01 42 96 14 88

Australian Embassy and Consulate 4 Rue Jean-Rey, 75015 Paris. ☎ 01 40 59 33 00

British Embassy 35 Rue du Faubourg St-Honoré, 75008 Paris. ☎ 01 42 66 91 42

British Consulate 16 Rue d'Anjou, 75008 Paris.
☎ 01 42 66 06 68

Canadian Embassy 35 Avenue Montaigne, 75008 Paris.
☎ 01 44 43 29 00

Irish Embassy 4 Rue Rude, 75016 Paris. ☎ 01 45 00 20 87

New Zealand Embassy 7 ter
Rue Léonard-de-Vinci, 75016
Paris. ☎ 01 45 00 24 11

Crime

Being the victim of theft can
ruin a holiday, so take every
precaution to prevent this
happening to you. The best
advice is to be aware at all
times, carry as little money and
as few credit cards as possible,
and leave any valuables in the
hotel safe. Never leave your car
unlocked, and hide away or
remove items of value.

If you have anything stolen,
report it immediately to the
nearest police station (*Commis-
sariat de Police*), and collect a
report so that you can make an
insurance claim. If your pass-

The ruins of the 13C Hunaudaye Castle, between Dinan and St-Brieuc.

...ort is stolen, report it to the Consulate or Embassy at once.

Currency see **Money**

Customs and Entry Regulations see **Arriving** p.108

Disabled Visitors

The *Michelin Red Guide France* and *Michelin Camping Caravaning France* indicate which hotels and camp sites have facilities for disabled visitors. You can also get information on Minitel 3615 HANDITEL.

Holidays and Travel Abroad: A Guide to Europe is available from RADAR, 12 City Forum, 250 City Road, London EC1V 8AF ☎ 0171 250 3222. It contains advice and information about accommodation, transport, services, equipment and tour operators in France. You are advised to check facilities available at hotels and at sights you plan to visit in advance. The local tourist office will also be able to give you up-to-date advice. *See* **Tourist Information Offices**

Driving

Drivers in France should carry a full national driving licence if they are EU citizens, or an international driving licence if they are not, as well as insur-

ance documents including a green card (no longer compulsory for EU members but strongly recommended), registration papers for the car, and a nationality sticker for the rear of the car.

Headlight beams should be adjusted for right-hand drive, and you should also have a spare set of light bulbs. Full or dipped headlights should be switched on at night or in poor visibility.

The minimum age for driving in France is 18, and driving is on the right-hand side.

Front-seat passengers must wear seatbelts, and back-seat passengers must wear them where they are fitted. Children under ten must travel in the rear of the car.

Some traffic regulations are peculiar to France: for example, vehicles joining a road from the right have priority on all roads except those with a yellow diamond sign.

Those driving or speeding with a blood-alcohol over the legal maximum (0.5g/litre) can be dealt with harshly, usually by on-the-spot fines.

Speed limits are as follows: *Built-up areas* 50kph/31mph *Dual carriageways and motorways without tolls*

110kph/
68mph (if raining 100kph/
62mph)
Toll motorways
130kph/80mph (if raining
110kph/68mph)
Other roads 90kph/56mph
(if raining 80kph/50mph)
*Minimum speed limit on
outside lane of motorways in
good conditions*
80kph/50mph
For 24-hour road and route-
planning information
☎ 48 94 33 33. *See also*
Accidents and Breakdowns

Electric Current
The voltage in France – including on campsites – is usually
220V. Plugs and sockets vary
greatly, though, and adaptors
are generally required.

Embassies *see* **Consulates**

Emergencies
For an emergency requiring:
Police ☎ 17
Fire Brigade ☎ 18
Ambulance (Samu) ☎ 15
The Operator's number is 13,
and Directory Enquiries is 12.
In cases of emergency the
Consulate or Embassy might
offer limited help.
See **Consulates**

Etiquette
As in most places in the world,
it is considered polite and
respectful to cover up decently
in churches, museums,
theatres etc. The French are a
more formal people than the
British, shaking hands when
they meet and addressing each
other correctly by their title
when they are not over
familiar. Thus 'Bonjour
Madame/Monsieur' should
begin any conversation with a
shopkeeper, post office clerk
or hotel desk staff, etc.

Excursions
The coast and countryside of
Brittany are particularly interesting, and there are some
unique and unusual places to
visit. Trips in old-fashioned
sailing ships are available, and
many lighthouses and beacons
along the coast – the highest
concentration in France – are
open to tourists.

The Channel and the
Atlantic are linked by river and
canal, and relaxing cruises on
these inland waterways can be
enjoyed. Details of these and
many other tours and excursions are available from the
various tourist offices which
can be found throughout
Brittany. For details *see* **Tourist
Information Offices**.

Guidebooks *see* **Maps**

Health

UK nationals should carry a form E111 (forms available from post offices) which is produced by the Department of Health, and which entitles the holder to free urgent treatment for accident or illness in EU countries. The treatment will have to be paid for in the first instance, but can be reclaimed later. All foreign nationals are advised to take out comprehensive insurance cover, and to keep any bills, receipts and invoices to support any claim.

Lists of doctors can be obtained from hotels, chemists or police stations, and first aid and medical advice is also available at pharmacies (look out for the green cross outside). The latter are generally open from 2–7.30pm, Monday, 9am–7.30pm, Tuesday to Saturday, and those which are open late or on Sundays display notices on their doors.

Information see
Tourist Information Offices

Language

The Breton language is still spoken, along with French, in the extreme west of Brittany,

This traditional fishing vessel is now a tourist boat.

and owes its origins to Irish and Welsh. Your efforts to speak French will be much appreciated everywhere, and even a few simple words and expressions are often warmly received. Below are a few words and phrases to help you make the most of your stay.

Laundry

Self-service, coin-operated launderettes can be easily found in tourist resorts, towns and cities throughout Brittany, as well as on larger campsites. Chain dry cleaners offer a quick and cheap service, but are not always recommended for delicate clothes. Many hotels provide a laundry and dry-cleaning service.

Lost Property

Airports and major railway stations have their own lost property offices (*Objets trouvés*) and if something goes missing in your hotel check with the front desk and hotel security. Report all lost or stolen items to the police, and always be sure to get a report to substantiate any insurance claims.

Should you lose any travel documents, contact the police, and in the event of a passport going missing, inform your

---

Good morning / **Bonjour**
Goodbye / **Au revoir**
Yes/no / **Oui/non**
Please/thank you / **S'il vous plaît/merci**
Sorry / **Pardon**
Do you speak English? / **Parlez-vous anglais?**
I want to buy / **Je voudrais acheter**
How much is it? / **Quel est le prix?**
The bill, please / **L'addition, s'il vous plaît**
I'd like a booklet of tickets / **Je voudrais un carnet**
Is service included? / **Le service est-il compris?**
Black espresso / **Un café**
White coffee / **Un café au lait/crème**
Fresh lemon or orange juice / **Un citron pressé ou une orange pressée**
A bottled beer / **Une bouteille de bière**
A draught beer / **Une bière pression**

Embassy or Consulate immediately (*see* **Consulates**).

Lost or stolen travellers' cheques and credit cards should be reported immediately to the issuing company with a list of numbers, and the police should be informed.

Maps

Michelin produce a complete range of maps for the traveller in Brittany. *Regional Map* No. 230 covers the area, while No. 58 Brest-Quimper-St Brieuc, No. 59 St-Brieuc-St-Malo-Rennes and No. 63 Vannes-La Baule-Angers are more detailed. *Michelin Green Guide Brittany* contains full information on the sights and attractions in the region.

Medical Care *see* Health

Money

The French unit of currency is the franc, which is divided into 100 centimes. Bank notes are issued in denominations of 500F, 200F, 100F, 50F and 20F, while coins come in 20F, 10F, 5F, 2F, 1F and 50c (all silver apart from the 20F and 10F coins which have a bronze border and an older bronze-coloured 10F coin), and the bronze-coloured 20c, 10c and 5c coins.

There are no restrictions on the amount of currency visitors can take into France, but perhaps the safest way to carry large amounts of money is in travellers' cheques which are widely accepted and exchanged. Bureaux de change are found at airports, terminals and larger railway stations, and at banks (*see also* **Banks**).

Exchange rates vary, so it pays to shop around. American Express, Carte Bleue (Visa/Barclaycard), Diners Club and Eurocard (Mastercard/Access) are widely accepted in shops, hotels and restaurants, motorways, petrol stations and many hypermarkets. Always check the amount which appears on the receipt, and note that in France there is no decimal point between francs and centimes, although a comma is often used.

Lost or stolen travellers' cheques and credit cards should be reported immediately to the issuing company with a list of numbers, and the police should also be informed.

Newspapers

In the main towns and cities of Brittany, English-language newspapers are widely available. You can buy them at pavement news kiosks, bookshops and drugstores. French daily newspapers include *Le Monde* and *Le Figaro*, and local papers such as *Ouest-France* and *le Télégramme de Brest*.

Opening Hours

The big **stores** and larger **shops** are generally open from 9am–6.30/7.30pm, Monday to Saturday. Some food shops open on Sunday mornings – bakers, for example – and close on Mondays, and they may close from noon–2pm for lunch. Opening hours are usually 7am–6.30pm, while hypermarkets stay open until 9pm or 10pm.

Chemists are generally open 2–7.30pm Monday, 9am–7.30pm Tuesday to Saturday, and some open later and on Sundays. Gendarmeries will give you their addresses (*see also* **Banks and Post Offices**).

Museums and monuments are generally open from 10am–5pm or 5.30pm, often with a break for lunch. Closing day is Tuesday for national museums and art galleries, and Monday for municipal museums.

Photography

Good-quality film and camera equipment are available everywhere in Brittany, and there are facilities for fast processing in larger towns.

Before taking photographs in museums and art galleries it would be wise to check with staff as photography is usually restricted in these places. In some instances hand-held cameras are admitted free, while payment is required for tripods and flashes are forbidden.

Police

In towns and cities, French police wear a dark blue uniform and a flat cap, and are known as the *Police Municipale*, while in country areas and small towns they are *Gendarmes*, and wear blue trousers, dark blue jackets and white belts. They are all generally courteous to tourists and in emergencies can be contacted on ☎ 17. Police can impose and collect on-the-spot fines for drivers who violate traffic regulations.

Post Offices

Post offices are open Monday to Friday, 8am–7pm, and Saturday 8am–noon. Some are also open at other times but only offer a limited service. Stamps are also available from newsagents and tobacconists, and some hotels.

Air mail letters and post

Sign outside a post office.

cards to the UK cost 3F; aero-
grammme (20g) to the USA
5F, letter or postcard to the
USA 4.40F, and a letter (20g)
to Australia and New Zealand
5.20F.

Poste restante mail should
be sent to the person at Poste
Restante, Post Centrale, postal
code of *département* followed by
town name, France, and a
passport should be taken along
as proof of identity when
collecting mail.

Public Holidays
New Year's Day: 1 January
Easter Sunday and Monday
   (*Pâques*)
Labour Day: 1 May
VE Day: 8 May
Ascension Day: 40 days after
   Easter
Whitsun (*Pentecôte*): 7th Sunday
   and Monday after Easter

Bastille Day: 14 July
Assumption Day: 15 August
All Saints' Day (*Toussaint*):
   1 November
Remembrance Day:
   11 November
Christmas Day: 25 December

Religion
France is largely a Roman-
Catholic country, with the
other major religions and
denominations often repre-
sented in larger towns and
cities. For particular details of
churches, chapels, synagogues
and mosques, enquire at any
tourist office (*see* **Tourist Information Offices**).

Smoking
Tabacs, the licensed tobacconists displaying red carrot-
shaped signs, sell cigarettes
and pipe tobacco, but these
are also on sale at drugstores
and certain restaurants and
bars. French brands like
Gauloises cost between 10–13F,
while English and American
cigarettes are dearer at 15–20F.

Telephones
Many public telephones take
phonecards (*télécartes*) which
can be bought from post
offices, tobacconists, newsagents, and at outlets adver-
tized on telephone booths.
Cards cost around 50F for 50

123

units, and around 100F for 120 units.

All numbers in the North-West begin with 02, those in Paris begin with 01, in the North-East with 03, in the South-East with 04 and in the South-West with 05. You do not have to dial these area codes if you are dialing within the same area.

To call abroad from France, first dial 00 and wait until the continuous tone recurs, then dial 44 plus STD code (minus the first 0) followed by the number for the UK, 61 for Australia, 1 for Canada and the USA, 64 for New Zealand and 353 for Eire.

Cheap rates with up to 65 per cent extra time are between 9pm–8am, Monday to Friday, and at weekends from noon on Saturday. Calls can be received at phone boxes which show the blue bell sign.

Emergency numbers

Fire ☎ 18; Police ☎ 17; Ambulance (*Samu*) ☎ 15; Operator ☎ 13; Directory Enquiries ☎ 12. For international enquiries ☎ 00 33 12 plus country code.

Time Difference

French standard time is GMT plus one hour. French summer time begins on the last Sunday in March at 2am when the clocks go forward an hour (the same day as British Summer Time), and ends on the last Sunday in September at 3am when the clocks go back (one month before BST ends).

Tipping

In France a 15 per cent service charge is usually included in the bill at hotels and restaurants, so there is no need to leave a tip; if you pay by cash it is considered polite to leave the small change for the waiter.

Public lavatory attendants with saucers may be happy with a few coins, but sometimes the price is displayed and is not negotiable. Tipping of 15 per cent is normal for taxi drivers, but not obligatory. There is no tipping in theatres.

A loose guide for tipping is: Hotel porter, per bag 5F. Hotel maid, per week 50–100F. Lavatory attendant 4F.

Toilets

Public conveniences can be found at railway and bus stations, in public buildings and in department stores.

Tourist Information Offices

The French Government Tourist Office is an excellent first source of information on everything from where to stay, to what to do on wet days.

Offices are at the following addresses:

UK 178 Piccadilly, London W1V 0AL ☎ 0891 244123 (brochures) ☎ 0171 629 2869 (information).

Australia BNP Building, 12 Castlereagh Street, Sydney, NSW 2000 ☎ 612 231 5244.

Canada 1981 Avenue McGill College, Suite 490, Esso Tower, Montreal, Quebec, H3A 2 W9 ☎ 514 288 4264.

USA France on Call Hotline: ☎ 900 990 0040 (\$.50 per minute) for information on hotels, restaurants and transportation.

East Coast – 444 Madison Avenue, New York 10020-10022 ☎ 212 838 7800.

Mid West – 676 North Michigan Avenue, Suite 3360, Chicago, IL 60611 ☎ 312 751 7800.

West Coast – 9454 Wilshire Boulevard, Suite 715 Beverley Hills, CA 90212 ☎ 310 271 2693.

Local tourist offices can be found at:

Comité départemental de Tourisme de l'Ille-et-Vilaine 4 Rue Jean-Jaurès, 35000 Rennes. ☎ 02 99 02 97 43

Comité départemental de Tourisme de Loire-Atlantique Maison du Tourisme, Place du

Children parade in traditional costume, Quimper.

Commerce, 44000 Nantes.
☎ 02 40 89 50 77
**Comité départemental de
Tourisme des Côtes-d'Armor**
29 Rue des Promenades,
BP 4620, 22046 St Brieuc
Cedex 2. ☎ 02 96 62 72 00
**Comité départemental de
Tourisme du Finistère** 11 Rue
Théodore-Le-Hars, BP 1419,
29104 Quimper Cedex.
☎ 02 98 53 09 00
**Comité départemental de
Tourisme du Morbihan** Hôtel
du Département, BP 400,
56009 Vannes Cedex.
☎ 02 97 54 06 56

Tourist information centres
(*Offices de tourisme*) can be
found in most large towns, and
they are well stocked with
leaflets providing information
on excursions, transport,
entertainment, facilities for the
disabled, and exhibitions, as
well as accommodation and
restaurants.

Transport
The French railway system
(SNCF) operates an extensive
network throughout France,
including many high-speed
trains (TGV) and motorail
services. There are so many
different ways of buying
reduced-price tickets that you
should enquire at a French
Tourist Office in your own
country for details before travelling, or at the tourist information centres or SNCF office
in France.

The SNCF also run bus
services between railway
stations and the surrounding
areas. Most larger towns have a
bus service, and you will find
that many country areas have a
reasonable, if infrequent,
service.

There are taxi ranks (*tête de
station*) outside railway stations
and in town centres. Taxis can
also be hailed in the street, or
you can order one by telephone.

TV and Radio
Some French hotels have TV
lounges, and some have TVs in
the bedrooms. All programmes
– apart from a few late-night
ones – are in French, but
English programmes are
broadcast on the radio in
summer, and BBC stations can
be picked up easily on short or
medium-wave radios.

Vaccinations
see **Before You Go p.108**

Water
Water served in hotels and
restaurants is perfectly safe to
drink, as is tap water unless
labelled *eau non potable* (not
drinking water).

INDEX

This index includes entries in both English (where used in the guide) and in French (*italics*).

Abbaye de Beauport 78
Abbaye de Bon-Repos 60
Aiguilles de Port-Coton 52
Alain 12
Aleth Coast Path 71
Alignements de Lagatjar 91
Alignements du Ménec 46
Amphitheatre 63
Ancenis 31
Antrain 35
Archéoscope 26
Armorique Regional Nature Park 63, 88, 98
Artu's Camp 62
Audierne 96
Auray 45

Baie des Trépassés 22, 96
Bais 35
Barenton Fountain 57
Barnenez Tumulus 82
Batz Island 86
Bay of the Dead 22
Beauport Abbey 78
Beg-Meil 52
Belle-Île 51, 102
Bertrand Du Guesclin 12, 13
Binic 77
Bonne-Fontaine Castle 35
Brasparts 66
Bréhat Island 78, 84
Brest 98
   Castle 98
   Museum Maritime 98
   Museum of Old Brest 98
   Océanopolis 98
   Tanguy Tower 98
Brière Regional Nature Park 23, 40, 102

Caesar's Mound 44
Cairn de Banenez 82
Cairn de Gavrinis 43
Calendar of Events 101
Camaret-sur-Mer 90, 102
Camp d'Artus 63
Cancale 68, 69
   Oyster and Shellfish Museum 68
Cape Fréhel 74, 75
Carantec 84
   Priest's Chair 84

Carhaix-Plouguer 62
   House of the Seneschal 62
Carnac 22, 46, 102
   Museum of Prehistory 47
   Plage 47
Cathedrale St-Tugdual 79
Channel Coast 10
Chaos du Moulin 63
Charlemagne 12
Charles de Bois 14
Châteaux:
   de Bonne-Fontaine 35
   de Comper 57
   de l'Hermine 41
   de la Motte-Glain 35
   Rochers-Sévigné 30
   de Suscinio 44
   Vauban 91
Châteaubriant 31
Châteaulin 98
Church of St-Armel 67
Citadelle Vauban 51
Clisson 32
Combourg 36
   Castle 36
   Cat Tower 36
   Lantern House 36
Commana 63
Concarneau 50, 102
   Fishing Museum 50
   Musée de la Pêche 50
   Walled Town 50
Corniche d'Aleth 71
Côte d'Emeraude 68
Côte des Abers 86
Crozon 90
Crozon Peninsula 89

Daoulas 98
Devil's Grotto 63
Dinan 72, 74, 102
   Fête des Remparts 73
   Pont Gothique 73
Dinard 102
   Grand Beach 71
Dol-de-Bretagne 36
   cathedral 36
   museum 36
Douarnenez 99
   Port Museum 99
   Duchess Anne 15

Eckmühl Lighthouse 96
Écluse de Bon-Repos 60
Edict of Nantes 16
Elven Towers 53
Emerald Coast 68
Erquy 76
Étang au Duc 67
Étang Carcraon 35

Falguérec-en-Séné Nature Reserve 43
Finistère 10
Folgoët 102
Fontaine de Barenton 57
Forêt de Quénécan 61
Fort-la-Latte 74
Forteresse de Largoët 53
Fouesnant 52
Fougères 28
François I 15

Gargantua's Finger 74
Gavrinis 43
Gavrinis Tumulus 43
Grande Brière 40
Great War 18
Groix Island 48
Groix Island Museum 48
Grotte de l'Apothicairerie 52
Grotte du Diable 63
Guérande 14, 40
Guerche-de-Bretagne 31
Guerlédan Lake 60
Guingamp 84, 102

Hell's Mouth Chasm 97
Hennebont 52
Hinterland Heart 23
Huelgoat 62

Ile-aux-Moines 43
Ile d'Arz 43
Ile d'Ouessant 87
Ile de Batz 86
Ile de Groix 48
Ile de Sein 96
Ile Molene 87
International Museum of Cape Horn Vessels 71

Jacques Cartier 16
Jean de Montfort 14
Josselin 58
   Castle 23
Jugon-les-Lacs 84

Kerjean Castle 99
Kernascléden 66, 67

La Baule 23, 38, 39, 102
La Conquet 87
La Maison des Artisans 66
La Roche-Maurice 88
La-Roche-Bernard 54
La-Roche-aux-Fées 30, 31
Lac de Guerlédan 60
Lagatjar Alignments 91
Lake Carcraon 35
Lamballe 85

INDEX

Larmor-Baden 43
Landerneau 88
Lannion 85
Largoët Castle 53
Le Bourg 84
Le Croisic 39, 40
Le Folgoët 99
Le Pallet 32
Le Pouldu 49
Le Pouliguen 40
Le Val-André 76
Les Forges-des-Salles 61
Les Montagnes Noires 62
Locronan 92, 93
Loctudy 96
Logan Stone 62
Logis Tiphaine 28
Loguivy de-la-Mer 78
Lorient 102
Louis XIV 16

Machecoul 54
Maison des Marmousets 67
Maison du Parc 89
Maison Marie Henri 49
Malansac 60
  Prehistoric Park 60
Malestroit 59
Ménec Alignments 46
Ménez-Hom 90 91
Merlin's Step 57
Mill Rocks 63
Mont-Dol 36
Moncontour 66
Mont-St-Michel 22, 26, 27
  abbey 26
Morbihan Gulf 25, 43
Morlaix 24, 82
Mur-de-Bretagne 61

Nantes 32, 103
  Botanical Gardens 35
  Ducal Castle 34
  Museums:
    Fine Arts 35
    Jules Verne 35
    Local Folk Art 35
  St Peter's and St Paul's
    Cathedral 33, 34
Noires Mountains 62
Nominoë 12
Notre-Dame-du-Haut 18

Paimpol 78, 103
  Maritime Museum 78
Paimpont 56, 103
Palais 51
Parish Closes 24, 64-65
Perron de Merlin 57
Perros-Guirec 24, 80, 103

Pink Granite Coast 68
Plage Bonaparte 78
Plage des Sables Blancs 51
Planétarium du Trégor 82
Pléhérel-Plage 75
Pleyben 64
Ploërmel 67
Plougastel Peninsula 99
Plougrescant 79
Ploumanach Beach 80
Pointe des Poulains 52
Pointe du Raz 96
Pont l'Abbé 96
  Bigouden Museum 96
Pont-Aven 49, 50, 103
Pontivy 60, 61
Pornic 53
Pornichet 40
Port-Coton Needles 52
Port-Louis 47
Presqu'île de Crozon 89
Presqu'île de Plougastel 99

Quénécan Forest 61
Quiberon 54
Quiberon Peninsula 22
Quimper 23, 24, 93, 103
  Museums:
    Faïence 95
    Fine Art 94
    Folk 95
Quimperlé 48
Quintin 67

Radar Dome and Telecommu-
  nications Museum 82
Raz Point 23, 96
Redon 37
Renaissance 16
Rennes 37
  Mordelaises Gate 37
  Museum of Brittany 37
  Museum of Fine Arts 37
  Thabor Gardens 37
Roc de Toulaëron 62
Roc Trévezel 63
Roche Tremblante 62
Rochefort-en-Terre 59

Roscoff 86
  Charles Pérez Aquarium 86
  Roch-Hievec Tropical Gar-
    dens 86
Rothéneuf Haven 68
  Sculptured Rocks 68, 69

Sables d'Or-les-Pins 75
Second World War 19
Sein Island 96
Sillon de Talbert 79

Sir Charles Chandos 14
Sizun 89
St-Briac-sur-Mer 85
St-Brieuc 74, 76
  St-Stephen's Cathedral 77
St-Cast-le-Guildo 74
St-Jacut-de-la-Mer 74
St-Jean-du-Doigt 85
St-Malo 17, 25, 68
  Castle 70
  Museum of Local History
    and Ethnography 70
  St-Vincent Cathedral 70
St-Marcel 59
  Museum of Breton Resis-
    tance 59
St-Mathieu Point 87, 88
St-Michael Tumulus 46
St-Pol-de-Léon 86
  cathedral 86
St-Quay-Portrieux 78
St-Servan-sur-Mer 71
St-Thégonnec 64
St-Tugdual Cathedral 79
Ste Suzanne Chapel 61
Ste-Anne d'Auray 45, 103
Suscinio Castle 44

Talbert Spit 79
Théâtre de Verdure 63
Trébeurden 81
Trégastel Plage 80,82
Trégor Planetarium 82
Tréguier 79
Tréhorenteuc 57
Trépassés Bay 96
Troménies 93

Ushant 87

Val sans Retour 57
Vallet 32
Vally of No Return 57
Vannes 25, 40, 103
  Automata Centre 41
  Constable Tower 42
  House of Vannes 43
  La Cohue 43
  Live Butterfly Centre 41
  Morbihan Archaeological
    Museum 43
  Oceanographic and Tropical
    Aquarium 41
  Prison Gate 43
  ramparts 42
  St Peter's Cathedral 42
  wash-houses 43
Vitré 29

Wars of Religion 16